D1077541

OLD MOORE'S

Horoscope and Astral Diary

PISCES

OLD MOORE'S

HOROSCOPE AND ASTRAL DIARY

PISCES

foulsham
LONDON • NEW YORK • TORONTO • SYDNEY

W. Foulsham & Co. Ltd

for Foulsham Publishing Ltd
The Old Barrel Store, Drayman's Lane, Marlow, Bucks SL7 2FF

Foulsham books can be found in all good bookshops and direct from
www.foulsham.com

ISBN: 978-0-572-04638-5

Copyright © 2016 Foulsham Publishing Ltd

A CIP record for this book is available from the British Library

Printed in Denmark by Nørhaven, Viborg

CONTENTS

INTRODUCTION

Astrology has been a part of life for centuries now, and no matter how technological our lives become, it seems that it never diminishes in popularity. For thousands of years people have been gazing up at the star-clad heavens and seeing their own activities and proclivities reflected in the movement of those little points of light. Across centuries countless hours have been spent studying the way our natures, activities and decisions seem to be paralleled by their predictable movements. Old Moore, a time-served veteran in astrological research, continues to monitor the zodiac and has produced the Astral Diary for 2017, tailor-made to your own astrological makeup.

Old Moore's Astral Diary is unique in its ability to get the heart of your nature and to offer you the sort of advice that might come from a trusted friend. It enables you to see in a day-by-day sense exactly how the planets are working for you. The diary section advises how you can get the best from upcoming situations and allows you to plan ahead successfully. There's also room on each daily entry to record your own observations or appointments.

While other popular astrology books merely deal with your astrological 'Sun sign', the Astral Diaries go much further. Every person on the planet is unique and Old Moore allows you to access your individuality in a number of ways. The front section gives you the chance to work out the placement of the Moon at the time of your birth and to see how its position has set an important seal on your overall nature. Perhaps most important of all, you can use the Astral Diary to discover your Rising Sign. This is the zodiac sign that was appearing over the Eastern horizon at the time of your birth and is just as important to you as an individual as is your Sun sign.

It is the synthesis of many different astrological possibilities that makes you what you are and with the Astral Diaries you can learn so much. How do you react to love and romance? Through the unique Venus tables and the readings that follow them, you can learn where the planet Venus was at the time of your birth. It is even possible to register when little Mercury is 'retrograde', which means that it appears to be moving backwards in space when viewed from the Earth. Mercury rules communication, so be prepared to deal with a few setbacks in this area when you see the sign ☿. The Astral Diary will be an interest and a support throughout the whole year ahead.

Old Moore extends his customary greeting to all people of the Earth and offers his age-old wishes for a happy and prosperous period ahead.

THE ESSENCE OF PISCES

Exploring the Personality of
Pisces the Fishes

(20TH FEBRUARY – 20TH MARCH)

What's in a sign?

Pisceans are fascinating people – everyone you come across is likely to admit that fact. By nature you are kind, loving, trustful and inclined to work very hard on behalf of the people you love – and perhaps even those you don't like very much. Your nature is sympathetic and you will do anything you can to improve the lot of those you consider to be worse off than yourself. There is a very forgiving side to your temperament and also a strong artistic flair that can find an outlet in any one of a dozen different ways.

It's true you are difficult to know, and there is a very important reason for this. Your nature goes deep, so deep in fact that someone would have to live with you for a lifetime to plumb even a part of its fathomless depths. What the world sees is only ever a small part of the total magic of this most compulsive and fascinating zodiac sign. Much of your latent power and natural magic is constantly kept bottled up, because it is never your desire to manipulate those around you. Rather, you tend to wait in the shadows until opportunities to come into your own present themselves.

In love you are ardent and sincere, though sometimes inclined to choose a partner too readily and too early. There's a dreamy quality to your nature that makes you easy to adore, but which can also cause difficulties if the practical necessities of life take a very definite second place.

The chances are that you love music and picturesque scenery, and you may also exhibit a definite fondness for animals. You prefer to live in the country rather than in the middle of a noisy and smelly town, and tend to keep a reasonably well-ordered household. Your family can easily become your life and you always need a focus for your energies. You are not at all good at feathering your own nest, unless you know that someone else is also going to benefit on the way. A little more selfishness probably would not go amiss on occasions because you are often far too willing to put yourself out wholesale for people who don't respect your sacrifices. Pisceans can be full of raging passions and are some of the most misunderstood people to be found anywhere within the great circle of the zodiac.

Pisces resources

It is the very essence of your zodiac sign that you are probably sitting there and saying to yourself 'Resources? I have no resources'. Of course you are wrong, though it has to be admitted that a glaring self-confidence isn't likely to be listed amongst them. You are, however, a very deep thinker, and this can turn out to be a great advantage and a useful tool when it comes to getting on in life. Because your natural intuition is so strong (some people would call you psychic), you are rarely fooled by the glib words of others. Your own natural tendency to tell the truth can be a distinct advantage and a great help to you when it comes to getting on in life from a practical and financial viewpoint.

Whilst many of the signs of the zodiac tend to respond to life in an impulsive way, you are more likely to weigh up the pros and cons of any given situation very carefully. This means that when you do take action you can achieve much more success – as well as saving a good deal of energy on the way. People tend to confide in you automatically, so you are definitely at an advantage when it comes to knowing what makes your family and friends tick. At work you can labour quietly and confidently, either on your own or in the company of others. Some people would assert that Pisceans are model employees because you really do not know how to give anything less than your best.

Never underestimate the power of your instincts. Under most circumstances you are aware of the possible outcome of any given situation and should react as your inner mind dictates. Following this course inevitably puts you ahead of the game and explains why so quiet a sign can promote so many winners in life. Not that you are particularly competitive. It's much more important for you to be part of a winning team than to be out there collecting the glory for yourself.

You are dependable, kind, loving and peerless in your defence of those you take to. All of these are incredible resources when used in the correct way. Perhaps most important of all is your ability to get others on your side. In this you cannot be matched.

Beneath the surface

Everyone instinctively knows that there is something very important going on beneath the surface of the Piscean mind, though working out exactly what it might be is a different kettle of fish altogether. The fact is that you are very secretive about yourself and tend to give very little away. There are occasions when this tendency can be a saving grace, but others where it is definitely a great disadvantage. What isn't hard to see is your natural sympathy and your desire to help those in trouble. There's no end gain here, it's simply the way you are. Your inspiration to do anything is rarely rooted in what your own prize is likely to be. In your soul you are poetical, deeply romantic and inextricably tied to the forces and cycles of the world that brought you to birth.

Despite your capacity for single-minded concentration in some matters, you are often subject to mental confusion. Rational considerations often take second place to intuitive foresight and even inspiration. Making leaps in logic isn't at all unusual for you and forms part of the way you judge the world and deal with it.

If you really want to get on in life, and to gain the most you can from your interactions with others, you need to be very truthful in your approach. Somehow or other that means finding out what is really going on in your mind and explaining it to those around you. This is never going to be an easy process, partly because of your naturally secretive ways. Actually some astrologers overplay the tendency of Pisces to keep its secrets. A great deal of the time you simply don't think you have anything to say that would interest others and you always lack confidence in your own judgements. This is a shame because you rarely proceed without thinking carefully and don't often make glaring mistakes.

Many Pisceans develop an ingrained tendency to believe themselves inadequate in some way. Once again this is something you should fight against. Knowing others better, and allowing them to get to know you, might cause you to feel less quirky or strange. Whether you realise it or not you have a natural magnetism that draws others towards you. Try to spend rather less time thinking – though without losing that Piscean ability to meditate which is central to your well-being. If you allow the fascinating world of the Piscean mind to be shared by the people you come to trust, you should become more understandable to people who really want to like you even more.

Making the best of yourself

It must be remembered that the zodiac sign of Pisces represents two Fishes, tethered by a cord but constantly trying to break away from each other. This says a great deal about the basic Piscean nature. The inward, contemplative side of your personality is often at odds with the more gregarious and chatty qualities you also possess. Learning about this duality of nature can go at least part of the way towards dealing with it.

Although you often exhibit a distinct lack of self-confidence in your dealings with the world at large, you are, at heart, quite adept, flexible and able to cope under almost any circumstance. All that is really required in order to have a positive influence on life and to be successful is for you to realise what you are capable of achieving. Alas this isn't quite as easy as it might appear, because the introspective depths of your nature make you think too much and cause you to avoid the very actions that would get you noticed more. This can be something of a dilemma for Pisces, though it is certainly not insurmountable.

Never be afraid to allow your sensitivity to show. It is one of your greatest assets and it is part of the reason why other people love you so much – far more, in fact, than you probably realise. Your natural warmth, grace and charm are certain to turn heads on those occasions when you can't avoid being watched. The creative qualities that you possess make it possible for you to manufacture harmonious surroundings, both for yourself and for your family, who are very important to you. At the same time you recognise the practical in life and don't mind getting your hands dirty, especially when it comes to helping someone else out of a mess.

One of the best ruses Pisceans can use in order to get over the innate shyness that often attends the sign is to put on an act. Pisceans are very good natural actors and can easily assume the role of another individual. So, in your dealings with the world at large, manufacture a more confident individual, though without leaving out all the wonderful things that make you what you are now. Play this part for all you are worth and you will then truly be making the best of yourself.

The impressions you give

There is absolutely no doubt that you are more popular, admired and even fancied than you could ever believe. Such is the natural modesty of your zodiac sign that you invariably fail to pick up on those little messages coming across from other people that say 'I think you are wonderful'. If we don't believe in ourselves it's difficult for us to accept that others think we are worth their consideration. Failing to realise your worth to the world at large is likely to be your greatest fault and needs to be corrected.

In a way it doesn't matter, when seen from the perspective of others. What they observe is a warm-hearted individual. Your magnetic personality is always on display, whether you intend it to be or not, which is another reason why you tend to attract far more attention than you would sometimes elicit. Most Pisceans are quite sexy, another quality that is bound to come across to the people you meet, at least some of whom would be willing to jump through hoops if you were to command it.

In short, what you show, and what you think you are, could be two entirely different things. If you don't believe this to be the case you need to carry out a straw poll amongst some of the people you know. Ask them to write down all your qualities as they see them. The result will almost certainly surprise you and demonstrate that you are far more capable, and loveable, than you believe yourself to be. Armed with this knowledge you can walk forward in life with more confidence and feel as content inside as you appear to be when viewed by the world at large.

People rely heavily on you. That much at least you will have noticed in a day-to-day sense. They do so because they know how well you deal with almost any situation. Even in a crisis you show your true colours and that's part of the reason why so many Piscean people find themselves involved in the medical profession. You are viewed as being stronger than you believe yourself to be, which is why everyone tends to be so surprised when they discover that you are vulnerable and inclined to worry.

The way forward

You have a great deal to offer the world, even if you don't always appreciate how much. Although you are capable of being shy and introverted on occasions, you are equally likely to be friendly, chatty and very co-operative. You settle to just about any task, though you do possess a sense of freedom that makes it difficult for you to be cooped up in the same place for days and weeks at a stretch. You prefer the sort of tasks that allow your own natural proclivities to shine out, and you exhibit an instinctive creative tendency in almost anything you do.

Use your natural popularity to the full. People are always willing to put themselves out on your behalf, mainly because they know how generous you are and want to repay you for some previous favour. You should never be too proud to accept this sort of proffered help and must avoid running away with the idea that you are unequal to any reasonable task that you set yourself.

It's true that some of your thoughts are extremely deep and that you can get yourself into something of a brown study on occasions, which can be translated by the world around you as depression. However, you are far more stable than you probably believe yourself to be because Pisces is actually one of the toughest of the zodiac signs.

Because you are born of a Water sign it is likely that you would take great delight in living near the sea, or some other large body of water. This isn't essential to your well-being but it does feed your imagination. The vastness of nature in all its forms probably appeals to you in any case and most Pisceans love the natural world with its staggering diversity.

In love you are ardent and sincere, but you do need to make sure that you choose the right individual to suit you. Pisceans often settle for a protecting arm, but if this turns out to be stifling, trouble could follow. You would find it hard to live with anyone who didn't have at least a degree of your sensitivity, and you need a partner who will allow you to retain that sense of inner freedom that is so vital to your well-being.

Make the most of the many gifts and virtues that nature has bestowed upon you and don't be afraid to let people know what you really are. Actually establishing this in the first place isn't easy for you. Pisceans respond well to almost any form of meditation, which is not surprising because the sign of the Fishes is the most spiritually motivated zodiac sign of them all. When you know yourself fully you generate a personality that is an inspiration to everyone.

PISCES ON THE CUSP

Old Moore is often asked how astrological profiles are altered for those people born at either the beginning or the end of a zodiac sign, or, more properly, on the cusps of a sign. In the case of Pisces this would be on the 20th of February and for two or three days after, and similarly at the end of the sign, probably from the 18th to the 20th of March. In this year's Astral Diaries, once again, Old Moore sets out to explain the differences regarding cuspid signs.

The Aquarius Cusp – February 20th to 22nd

This tends to be a generally happy combination of signs, even if some of the people you come into contact with find you rather difficult to understand from time to time. You are quite capable of cutting a dash, as any Aquarian would be, and yet at the same time you have the quiet and contemplative qualities more typified by Pisces. You tend to be seen as an immensely attractive person, even if you are the last one in the world to accept this fact. People find you to be friendly, very approachable and good company in almost any social or personal setting. It isn't hard for you to get on with others, though since you are not so naturally quiet as Pisces when taken alone, you are slightly more willing to speak your mind and to help out, though usually in a very diplomatic manner.

At work you are very capable and many people with this combination find themselves working on behalf of humanity as a whole. Thus work in social services, hospitals or charities really suits the unique combinations thrown up by this sign mixture. Management is right up your street, though there are times when your conception of popularity takes the foremost place in your mind. Occasionally this could take the edge off executive decisions. A careful attention to detail shows you in a position to get things done, even jobs that others shun. You don't really care for getting your hands dirty but will tackle almost any task if you know it to be necessary. Being basically self-sufficient, you also love the company of others, and it is this adaptability that is the hallmark of success to Aquarian-cusp Pisceans.

Few people actually know you as well as they think they do because the waters of your nature run quite deep. Your real task in life is to let the world know how you feel, something you fight shy of doing now and again. There are positive gains in your life, brought about as a result of your adaptable and pleasing nature. Aquarius present in the nature allows Pisces to act at its best.

The Aries Cusp – March 18th to 20th

This is a Piscean with attitude and probably one of the most difficult zodiac sign combinations to be understood, not only by those people with whom you come into contact but clearly by yourself too. If there are any problems thrown up here they come from the fact that Pisces and Aries have such different ways of expressing themselves to the world at large. Aries is very upfront, dynamic and dominant, all factors that are simply diametrically opposed to the way Pisces thinks and behaves. So the real task in life is to find ways to combine the qualities of Pisces and Aries, in a way that suits the needs of both and without becoming totally confused with regard to your basic nature.

The problem is usually solved by a compartmentation of life. For example, many people with this combination will show the Aries qualities strongly at work, whilst dropping into the Piscean mode socially and at home. This may invariably be the case but there are bound to be times when the underlying motivations become mixed, which can confuse those with whom you come into contact.

Having said all of this you can be the least selfish and most successful individual when you are fighting for the rights of others. This is the zodiac combination of the true social reformer, the genuine politician and the committed pacifist. It seems paradoxical to suggest that someone could fight tenaciously for peace, but this is certainly true in your case. You have excellent executive skills and yet retain an ability to tell other people what they should be doing, in fairly strident terms, usually without upsetting anyone. There is a degree of genuine magic about you that makes you very attractive and there is likely to be more than one love affair in your life. A steadfast view of romance may not be naturally present within your basic nature but like so much else you can 'train' this quality into existence.

Personal success is likely, but it probably doesn't matter all that much in a material sense. The important thing to you is being needed by the world at large.

PISCES AND ITS ASCENDANTS

The nature of every individual on the planet is composed of the rich variety of zodiac signs and planetary positions that were present at the time of their birth. Your Sun sign, which in your case is Pisces, is one of the many factors when it comes to assessing the unique person you are. Probably the most important consideration, other than your Sun sign, is to establish the zodiac sign that was rising over the eastern horizon at the time that you were born. This is your Ascending or Rising sign. Most popular astrology fails to take account of the Ascendant, and yet its importance remains with you from the very moment of your birth, through every day of your life. The Ascendant is evident in the way you approach the world, and so, when meeting a person for the first time, it is this astrological influence that you are most likely to notice first. Our Ascending sign essentially represents what we appear to be, while the Sun sign is what we feel inside ourselves.

The Ascendant also has the potential for modifying our overall nature. For example, if you were born at a time of day when Pisces was passing over the eastern horizon (this would be around the time of dawn) then you would be classed as a double Pisces. As such, you would typify this zodiac sign, both internally and in your dealings with others. However, if your Ascendant sign turned out to be a Fire sign, such as Aries, there would be a profound alteration of nature, away from the expected qualities of Pisces.

One of the reasons why popular astrology often ignores the Ascendant is that it has always been rather difficult to establish. Old Moore has found a way to make this possible by devising an easy-to-use table, which you will find on page 125 of this book. Using this, you can establish your Ascendant sign at a glance. You will need to know your rough time of birth, then it is simply a case of following the instructions.

For those readers who have no idea of their time of birth it might be worth allowing a good friend, or perhaps your partner, to read through the section that follows this introduction. Someone who deals with you on a regular basis may easily discover your Ascending sign, even though you could have some difficulty establishing it for yourself. A good understanding of this component of your nature is essential if you want to be aware of that 'other person' who is responsible for the way you make contact with the world at large. Your Sun sign, Ascendant sign, and the other pointers in this book will, together, allow you a far better understanding of what makes you tick as an individual. Peeling back the different layers of your astrological make-up can be an enlightening experience, and the Ascendant may represent one of the most important layers of all.

Pisces with Pisces Ascendant

You are a kind and considerate person who would do almost anything to please the people around you. Creative and extremely perceptive, nobody knows the twists and turns of human nature better than you do, and you make it your business to serve humanity in any way you can. Not everyone understands what makes you tick, and part of the reason for this state of affairs is that you are often not really quite 'in' the world as much as the people you encounter in a day-to-day sense. At work you are generally cheerful, though you can be very quiet on occasions, but since you are consistent in this regard, you don't attract adverse attention or accusations of being moody, as some other variants of Pisces sometimes do. Confusion can beset you on occasions, especially when you are trying to reconcile your own opposing needs. There are certain moments of discontent to be encountered which so often come from trying to please others, even when to do so goes against your own instincts.

As age and experience add to your personal armoury you relax more with the world and find yourself constantly sought out for words of wisdom. The vast majority of people care for you deeply.

Pisces with Aries Ascendant

Although not an easy combination to deal with, the Pisces with an Aries Ascendant does bring something very special to the world in the way of natural understanding allied to practical assistance. It's true that you can sometimes be a dreamer, but there is nothing wrong with that as long as you have the ability to turn some of your wishes into reality, and this you are usually able to do, often for the sake of those around you. Conversation comes easily to you, though you also possess a slightly wistful and poetic side to your nature, which is attractive to the many people who call you a friend. A natural entertainer, you bring a sense of the comic to the often serious qualities of Aries, though without losing the determination that typifies the sign.

In relationships you are ardent, sincere and supportive, with a social conscience that sometimes finds you fighting the battles of the less privileged members of society. Family is important to you and this is a combination that invariably leads to parenthood. Away from the cut and thrust of everyday life you relax more fully, and think about matters more deeply than more typical Aries types might.

Pisces with Taurus Ascendant

You are clearly a very sensitive type of person and that sometimes makes it rather difficult for others to know how they might best approach you. Private and deep, you are nevertheless socially inclined on many occasions. However, because your nature is bottomless it is possible that some types would actually accuse you of being shallow. How can this come about? Well, it's simple really. The fact is that you rarely show anyone what is going on in the deepest recesses of your mind and so your responses can appear to be trite or even ill-considered. This is far from the truth, as those who are allowed into the 'inner sanctum' would readily admit. You are something of a sensualist, and relish staying in bed late and simply pleasing yourself for days on end. However, you have Taurean traits so you desire a tidy environment in which to live your usually long life.

You are able to deal with the routine aspects of life quite well and can be a capable worker once you are up and firing on all cylinders. It is very important that you maintain an interest in what you are doing, because the recesses of your dreamy mind can sometimes appear to be infinitely more attractive. Your imagination is second to none and this fact can often be turned to your advantage.

Pisces with Gemini Ascendant

There is great duality inherent in this combination, and sometimes this can cause a few problems. Part of the trouble stems from the fact that you often fail to realise what you want from life, and you could also be accused of failing to take the time out to think things through carefully enough. You are reactive, and although you have every bit of the natural charm that typifies the sign of Gemini, you are more prone to periods of self-doubt and confusion. However, you should not allow these facts to get you down too much, because you are also genuinely loved and have a tremendous capacity to look after others, a factor which is more important to you than any other. It's true that personal relationships can sometimes be a cause of difficulty for you, partly because your constant need to know what makes other people tick could drive them up the wall. Accepting people at face value seems to be the best key to happiness of a personal sort, and there are occasions when your very real and natural intuition has to be put on hold.

It's likely that you are an original, particularly in the way you dress. An early rebellious stage often gives way to a more comfortable form of eccentricity. When you are at your best, just about everyone adores you.

Pisces with Cancer Ascendant

A deep, double Water-sign combination this, and it might serve to make you a very misunderstood, though undoubtedly popular, individual. You are anxious to make a good impression, probably too keen under certain circumstances, and you do everything you can to help others, even if you don't know them very well. It's true that you are deeply sensitive and quite easily brought to tears by the suffering of this most imperfect world that we inhabit. Fatigue can be a problem, though this is somewhat nullified by the fact that you can withdraw completely into the deep recesses of your own mind when it becomes necessary to do so.

You may not be the most gregarious person in the world, simply because it isn't easy for you to put some of your most important considerations into words. This is easier when you are in the company of people you know and trust, though even trust is a commodity that is difficult for you to find, particularly since you may have been hurt by being too willing to share your thoughts early in life. With age comes wisdom and maturity, and the older you are, the better you will learn to handle this potent and demanding combination. You will never go short of either friends or would-be lovers, and may be one of the most magnetic types of both Cancer and Pisces.

Pisces with Leo Ascendant

You are a very sensitive soul, on occasions too much so for your own good. However, there is not a better advocate for the rights of humanity than you represent and you constantly do what you can to support the downtrodden and oppressed. Good causes are your thing and there are likely to be many in your life. You will probably find yourself pushed to the front of almost any enterprise of which you are a part because, despite the deeper qualities of Pisces, you are a natural leader. Even on those occasions when it feels as though you lack confidence, you manage to muddle through somehow and your smile is as broad as the day. Few sign combinations are more loved than this one, mainly because you do not have a malicious bone in your body, and will readily forgive and forget, which the Lion on its own often will not.

Although you are capable of acting on impulse, you do so from a deep sense of moral conviction, so that most of your endeavours are designed to suit other people too. They recognise this fact and will push much support back in your direction. Even when you come across troubles in your life you manage to find ways to sort them out, and will invariably notice something new to smile about on the way. Your sensitivity rating is massive and you can easily be moved to tears.

Pisces with Virgo Ascendant

You might have been accused on occasions of being too sensitive for your own good, a charge that is not entirely without foundation. Certainly you are very understanding of the needs of others, sometimes to the extent that you put everything aside to help them. This would also be true in the case of charities, for you care very much about the world and the people who cling tenaciously to its surface. Your ability to love on a one-to-one basis knows no bounds, though you may not discriminate as much as you could, particularly when young, and might have one or two false starts in the love stakes. You don't always choose to verbalise your thoughts and this can cause problems, because there is always so much going on in your mind and Virgo especially needs good powers of communication. Pisces is quieter and you need to force yourself to say what you think when the explanation is important.

You would never betray a confidence and sometimes take on rather more for the sake of your friends than is strictly good for you. This is not a fault but can cause you problems all the same. Because you are so intuitive there is little that escapes your attention, though you should avoid being pessimistic about your insights. Changes of scenery suit you and travel would bring out the best in what can be a repressed nature.

Pisces with Libra Ascendant

An Air and Water combination, you are not easy to understand and have depths that show at times, surprising those people who thought they already knew what you were. You will always keep people guessing and are just as likely to hitchhike around Europe as you are to hold down a steady job, both of which you would undertake with the same degree of commitment and success. Usually young at heart, but always carrying the potential for an old head on young shoulders, you are something of a paradox and not at all easy for totally 'straight' types to understand. But you always make an impression, and tend to be very attractive to members of the opposite sex.

In matters of health you do have to be a little careful because you dissipate much nervous energy and can sometimes be inclined to push yourself too hard, at least in a mental sense. Frequent periods of rest and meditation will do you the world of good and should improve your level of wisdom, which tends to be fairly high already. Much of your effort in life is expounded on behalf of humanity as a whole, for you care deeply, love totally and always give of your best. Whatever your faults and failings might be, you are one of the most popular people around.

Pisces with Scorpio Ascendant

You stand a chance of disappearing so deep into yourself that other people would need one of those long ladders that cave explorers use to even find you. It isn't really your fault, because both Scorpio and Pisces, as Water signs, are difficult to understand and you have them both. But that doesn't mean that you should be content to remain in the dark, and the warmth of your nature is all you need to shine a light on the wonderful qualities you possess. But the primary word of warning is that you must put yourself on display and allow others to know what you are, before their appreciation of these facts becomes apparent.

As a server of the world you are second to none and it is hard to find a person with this combination who is not, in some way, looking out for the people around them. Immensely attractive to others, you are also one of the most sought-after lovers. Much of this has to do with your deep and abiding charm, but the air of mystery that surrounds you also helps. Some of you will marry too early, and end up regretting the fact, though the majority of people with Scorpio and Pisces will find the love they deserve in the end. You are able, just, firm but fair, though a sucker for a hard luck story and as kind as the day is long. It's hard to imagine how so many good points could be ignored by others.

Pisces with Sagittarius Ascendant

A very attractive combination this, because the more dominant qualities of the Archer are somehow mellowed-out by the caring Water-sign qualities of the Fishes. You can be very outgoing, but there is always a deeper side to your nature that allows others to know that you are thinking about them. Few people could fall out with either your basic nature or your attitude to the world at large, even though there are depths to your nature that may not be easily understood. You are capable, have a good executive ability and can work hard to achieve your objectives, even if you get a little disillusioned on the way. Much of your life is given over to helping those around you and there is a great tendency for you to work for and on behalf of humanity as a whole. A sense of community is brought to most of what you do and you enjoy co-operation. Although you have the natural ability to attract people to you, the Pisces half of your nature makes you just a little more reserved in personal matters than might otherwise be the case. More careful in your choices than either sign taken alone, you still have to make certain that your motivations when commencing a personal relationship are the right ones. You love to be happy, and to offer gifts of happiness to others.

Pisces with Capricorn Ascendant

You are certainly not the easiest person in the world to understand, mainly because your nature is so deep and your personality so complicated, that others are somewhat intimidated at the prospect of staring into this abyss. All the same your friendly nature is attractive, and there will always be people around who are fascinated by the sheer magnetic quality that is intrinsic to this zodiac mix. Sentimental and extremely kind, there is no limit to the extent of your efforts on behalf of a deserving world, though there are some people around who wonder at your commitment and who may ridicule you a little for your staying-power, even in the face of some adversity. At work you are very capable, will work long and hard, and can definitely expect a greater degree of financial and practical success than Pisces when taken alone. Routines don't bother you too much, though you do need regular periods of introspection, which help to recharge low batteries and a battered self-esteem. In affairs of the heart you are given to impulse, which belies the more careful qualities of Capricorn. However, the determination remains intact and you are quite capable of chasing rainbows round and round the same field, never realising that you can't get to the end of them. Generally speaking you are an immensely lovable person and a great favourite to many.

Pisces with Aquarius Ascendant

Here we find the originality of Aquarius balanced by the very sensitive qualities of Pisces, and it makes for a very interesting combination. When it comes to understanding other people you are second to none, but it's certain that you are more instinctive than either Pisces or Aquarius when taken alone. You are better at routines than Aquarius, but also relish a challenge more than the typical Piscean would. Active and enterprising, you tend to know what you want from life, but consideration of others, and the world at large, will always be part of the scenario. People with this combination often work on behalf of humanity and are to be found in social work, the medical profession and religious institutions. As far as beliefs are concerned you don't conform to established patterns, and yet may get closer to the truth of the Creator than many deep theological thinkers have ever been able to do. Acting on impulse as much as you do means that not everyone understands the way your mind works, but your popularity will invariably see you through.

Passionate and deeply sensitive, you are able to negotiate the twists and turns of a romantic life that is hardly likely to be run-of-the-mill. In the end, however, you should certainly be able to find a very deep personal and spiritual happiness.

THE MOON AND THE PART IT PLAYS IN YOUR LIFE

In astrology the Moon is probably the single most important heavenly body after the Sun. Its unique position, as partner to the Earth on its journey around the solar system, means that the Moon appears to pass through the signs of the zodiac extremely quickly. The zodiac position of the Moon at the time of your birth plays a great part in personal character and is especially significant in the build-up of your emotional nature.

Sun Moon Cycles

The first lunar cycle deals with the part the position of the Moon plays relative to your Sun sign. I have made the fluctuations of this pattern easy for you to understand by means of a simple cyclic graph. It appears on the first page of each 'Your Month At A Glance', under the title 'Highs and Lows'. The graph displays the lunar cycle and you will soon learn to understand how its movements have a bearing on your level of energy and your abilities.

Your Own Moon Sign

Discovering the position of the Moon at the time of your birth has always been notoriously difficult because tracking the complex zodiac positions of the Moon is not easy. This process has been reduced to three simple stages with Old Moore's unique Lunar Tables. A breakdown of the Moon's zodiac positions can be found from page 28 onwards, so that once you know what your Moon Sign is, you can see what part this plays in the overall build-up of your personal character.

If you follow the instructions on the next page you will soon be able to work out exactly what zodiac sign the Moon occupied on the day that you were born and you can then go on to compare the reading for this position with those of your Sun sign and your Ascendant. It is partly the comparison between these three important positions that goes towards making you the unique individual you are.

HOW TO DISCOVER YOUR MOON SIGN

This is a three-stage process. You may need a pen and a piece of paper but if you follow the instructions below the process should only take a minute or so.

STAGE 1 First of all you need to know the Moon Age at the time of your birth. If you look at Moon Table 1, on page 26, you will find all the years between 1919 and 2017 down the left side. Find the year of your birth and then trace across to the right to the month of your birth. Where the two intersect you will find a number. This is the date of the New Moon in the month that you were born. You now need to count forward the number of days between the New Moon and your own birthday. For example, if the New Moon in the month of your birth was shown as being the 6th and you were born on the 20th, your Moon Age Day would be 14. If the New Moon in the month of your birth came after your birthday, you need to count forward from the New Moon in the previous month. If you were born in a Leap Year, remember to count the 29th February. You can tell if your birth year was a Leap Year if the last two digits can be divided by four. Whatever the result, jot this number down so that you do not forget it.

STAGE 2 Take a look at Moon Table 2 on page 27. Down the left hand column look for the date of your birth. Now trace across to the month of your birth. Where the two meet you will find a letter. Copy this letter down alongside your Moon Age Day.

STAGE 3 Moon Table 3 on page 27 will supply you with the zodiac sign the Moon occupied on the day of your birth. Look for your Moon Age Day down the left hand column and then for the letter you found in Stage 2. Where the two converge you will find a zodiac sign and this is the sign occupied by the Moon on the day that you were born.

Your Zodiac Moon Sign Explained

You will find a profile of all zodiac Moon Signs on pages 28 to 31, showing in yet another way how astrology helps to make you into the individual that you are. In each daily entry of the Astral Diary you can find the zodiac position of the Moon for every day of the year. This also allows you to discover your lunar birthdays. Since the Moon passes through all the signs of the zodiac in about a month, you can expect something like twelve lunar birthdays each year. At these times you are likely to be emotionally steady and able to make the sort of decisions that have real, lasting value.

Moon Table 1

YEAR	JAN	FEB	MAR	YEAR	JAN	FEB	MAR	YEAR	JAN	FEB	MAR
1919	1/31	–	2/31	1952	26	25	25	1985	21	19	21
1920	21	19	20	1953	15	14	15	1986	10	9	10
1921	9	8	9	1954	5	3	5	1987	29	28	29
1922	27	26	28	1955	24	22	24	1988	18	17	18
1923	17	15	17	1956	13	11	12	1989	7	6	7
1924	6	5	5	1957	1/30	–	1/31	1990	26	25	26
1925	24	23	24	1958	19	18	20	1991	15	14	15
1926	14	12	14	1959	9	7	9	1992	4	3	4
1927	3	2	3	1960	27	26	27	1993	24	22	24
1928	21	19	21	1961	16	15	16	1994	11	10	12
1929	11	9	11	1962	6	5	6	1995	1/31	–	1/30
1930	29	28	30	1963	25	23	25	1996	19	18	19
1931	18	17	19	1964	14	13	14	1997	9	7	9
1932	7	6	7	1965	3	1	2	1998	27	26	27
1933	25	24	26	1966	21	19	21	1999	16	15	16
1934	15	14	15	1967	10	9	10	2000	6	4	6
1935	5	3	5	1968	29	28	29	2001	24	23	25
1936	24	22	23	1969	19	17	18	2002	13	12	13
1937	12	11	12	1970	7	6	7	2003	3	1	2
1938	1/31	–	2/31	1971	26	25	26	2004	21	20	21
1939	20	19	20	1972	15	14	15	2005	10	9	10
1940	9	8	9	1973	5	4	5	2006	29	28	29
1941	27	26	27	1974	24	22	24	2007	18	16	18
1942	16	15	16	1975	12	11	12	2008	8	6	7
1943	6	4	6	1976	1/31	29	30	2009	26	25	26
1944	25	24	24	1977	19	18	19	2010	15	14	15
1945	14	12	14	1978	9	7	9	2011	4	3	5
1946	3	2	3	1979	27	26	27	2012	23	22	22
1947	21	19	21	1980	16	15	16	2013	12	10	12
1948	11	9	11	1981	6	4	6	2014	1/31	–	1
1949	29	27	29	1982	25	23	24	2015	19	20	19
1950	18	16	18	1983	14	13	14	2016	9	8	8
1951	7	6	7	1984	3	1	2	2017	27	25	27

Table 2

DAY	FEB	MAR
1	D	F
2	D	G
3	D	G
4	D	G
5	D	G
6	D	G
7	D	G
8	D	G
9	D	G
10	E	G
11	E	G
12	E	H
13	E	H
14	E	H
15	E	H
16	E	H
17	E	H
18	E	H
19	E	H
20	F	H
21	F	H
22	F	I
23	F	I
24	F	I
25	F	I
26	F	I
27	F	I
28	F	I
29	F	I
30	–	I
31	–	I

Table 3

M/D	D	E	F	G	H	I	J
0	AQ	PI	PI	PI	AR	AR	AR
1	PI	PI	PI	AR	AR	AR	TA
2	PI	PI	AR	AR	AR	TA	TA
3	PI	AR	AR	AR	TA	TA	TA
4	AR	AR	AR	TA	TA	GE	GE
5	AR	TA	TA	TA	GE	GE	GE
6	TA	TA	TA	GE	GE	GE	CA
7	TA	TA	GE	GE	GE	CA	CA
8	TA	GE	GE	GE	CA	CA	CA
9	GE	GE	CA	CA	CA	CA	LE
10	GE	CA	CA	CA	LE	LE	LE
11	CA	CA	CA	LE	LE	LE	VI
12	CA	CA	LE	LE	LE	VI	VI
13	LE	LE	LE	LE	VI	VI	VI
14	LE	LE	VI	VI	VI	LI	LI
15	LE	VI	VI	VI	LI	LI	LI
16	VI	VI	VI	LI	LI	LI	SC
17	VI	VI	LI	LI	LI	SC	SC
18	VI	LI	LI	LI	SC	SC	SC
19	LI	LI	LI	SC	SC	SC	SA
20	LI	SC	SC	SC	SA	SA	SA
21	SC	SC	SC	SA	SA	SA	CP
22	SC	SC	SA	SA	SA	CP	CP
23	SC	SA	SA	SA	CP	CP	CP
24	SA	SA	SA	CP	CP	CP	AQ
25	SA	CP	CP	CP	AQ	AQ	AQ
26	CP	CP	CP	AQ	AQ	AQ	PI
27	CP	AQ	AQ	AQ	AQ	PI	PI
28	AQ	AQ	AQ	AQ	PI	PI	PI
29	AQ	AQ	AQ	PI	PI	PI	AR

AR = Aries, TA = Taurus, GE = Gemini, CA = Cancer, LE = Leo, VI = Virgo, LI = Libra, SC = Scorpio, SA = Sagittarius, CP = Capricorn, AQ = Aquarius, PI = Pisces

MOON SIGNS

Moon in Aries

You have a strong imagination, courage, determination and a desire to do things in your own way and forge your own path through life.

Originality is a key attribute; you are seldom stuck for ideas although your mind is changeable and you could take the time to focus on individual tasks. Often quick-tempered, you take orders from few people and live life at a fast pace. Avoid health problems by taking regular time out for rest and relaxation.

Emotionally, it is important that you talk to those you are closest to and work out your true feelings. Once you discover that people are there to help, there is less necessity for you to do everything yourself.

Moon in Taurus

The Moon in Taurus gives you a courteous and friendly manner, which means you are likely to have many friends.

The good things in life mean a lot to you, as Taurus is an Earth sign that delights in experiences which please the senses. Hence you are probably a lover of good food and drink, which may in turn mean you need to keep an eye on the bathroom scales, especially as looking good is also important to you.

Emotionally you are fairly stable and you stick by your own standards. Taureans do not respond well to change. Intuition also plays an important part in your life.

Moon in Gemini

You have a warm-hearted character, sympathetic and eager to help others. At times reserved, you can also be articulate and chatty: this is part of the paradox of Gemini, which always brings duplicity to the nature. You are interested in current affairs, have a good intellect, and are good company and likely to have many friends. Most of your friends have a high opinion of you and would be ready to defend you should the need arise. However, this is usually unnecessary, as you are quite capable of defending yourself in any verbal confrontation.

Travel is important to your inquisitive mind and you find intellectual stimulus in mixing with people from different cultures. You also gain much from reading, writing and the arts but you do need plenty of rest and relaxation in order to avoid fatigue.

Moon in Cancer

The Moon in Cancer at the time of birth is a fortunate position as Cancer is the Moon's natural home. This means that the qualities of compassion and understanding given by the Moon are especially enhanced in your nature, and you are friendly and sociable and cope well with emotional pressures. You cherish home and family life, and happily do the domestic tasks. Your surroundings are important to you and you hate squalor and filth. You are likely to have a love of music and poetry.

Your basic character, although at times changeable like the Moon itself, depends on symmetry. You aim to make your surroundings comfortable and harmonious, for yourself and those close to you.

Moon in Leo

The best qualities of the Moon and Leo come together to make you warmhearted, fair, ambitious and self-confident. With good organisational abilities, you invariably rise to a position of responsibility in your chosen career. This is fortunate as you don't enjoy being an 'also-ran' and would rather be an important part of a small organisation than a menial in a large one.

You should be lucky in love, and happy, provided you put in the effort to make a comfortable home for yourself and those close to you. It is likely that you will have a love of pleasure, sport, music and literature. Life brings you many rewards, most of them as a direct result of your own efforts, although you may be luckier than average and ready to make the best of any situation.

Moon in Virgo

You are endowed with good mental abilities and a keen receptive memory, but you are never ostentatious or pretentious. Naturally quite reserved, you still have many friends, especially of the opposite sex. Marital relationships must be discussed carefully and worked at so that they remain harmonious, as personal attachments can be a problem if you do not give them your full attention.

Talented and persevering, you possess artistic qualities and are a good homemaker. Earning your honours through genuine merit, you work long and hard towards your objectives but show little pride in your achievements. Many short journeys will be undertaken in your life.

Moon in Libra

With the Moon in Libra you are naturally popular and make friends easily. People like you, probably more than you realise, you bring fun to a party and are a natural diplomat. For all its good points, Libra is not the most stable of astrological signs and, as a result, your emotions can be a little unstable too. Therefore, although the Moon in Libra is said to be good for love and marriage, your Sun sign and Rising sign will have an important effect on your emotional and loving qualities.

You must remember to relate to others in your decision-making. Co-operation is crucial because Libra represents the 'balance' of life that can only be achieved through harmonious relationships. Conformity is not easy for you because Libra, an Air sign, likes its independence.

Moon in Scorpio

Some people might call you pushy. In fact, all you really want to do is to live life to the full and protect yourself and your family from the pressures of life. Take care to avoid giving the impression of being sarcastic or impulsive and use your energies wisely and constructively.

You have great courage and you invariably achieve your goals by force of personality and sheer effort. You are fond of mystery and are good at predicting the outcome of situations and events. Travel experiences can be beneficial to you.

You may experience problems if you do not take time to examine your motives in a relationship, and also if you allow jealousy, always a feature of Scorpio, to cloud your judgement.

Moon in Sagittarius

The Moon in Sagittarius helps to make you a generous individual with humanitarian qualities and a kind heart. Restlessness may be intrinsic as your mind is seldom still. Perhaps because of this, you have a need for change that could lead you to several major moves during your adult life. You are not afraid to stand your ground when you know your judgement is right, you speak directly and have good intuition.

At work you are quick, efficient and versatile and so you make an ideal employee. You need work to be intellectually demanding and do not enjoy tedious routines.

In relationships, you anger quickly if faced with stupidity or deception, though you are just as quick to forgive and forget. Emotionally, there are times when your heart rules your head.

Moon in Capricorn

The Moon in Capricorn makes you popular and likely to come into the public eye in some way. The watery Moon is not entirely comfortable in the Earth sign of Capricorn and this may lead to some difficulties in the early years of life. An initial lack of creative ability and indecision must be overcome before the true qualities of patience and perseverance inherent in Capricorn can show through.

You have good administrative ability and are a capable worker, and if you are careful you can accumulate wealth. But you must be cautious and take professional advice in partnerships, as you are open to deception. You may be interested in social or welfare work, which suit your organisational skills and sympathy for others.

Moon in Aquarius

The Moon in Aquarius makes you an active and agreeable person with a friendly, easy-going nature. Sympathetic to the needs of others, you flourish in a laid-back atmosphere. You are broad-minded, fair and open to suggestion, although sometimes you have an unconventional quality which others can find hard to understand.

You are interested in the strange and curious, and in old articles and places. You enjoy trips to these places and gain much from them. Political, scientific and educational work interests you and you might choose a career in science or technology.

Money-wise, you make gains through innovation and concentration and Lunar Aquarians often tackle more than one job at a time. In love you are kind and honest.

Moon in Pisces

You have a kind, sympathetic nature, somewhat retiring at times, but you always take account of others' feelings and help when you can.

Personal relationships may be problematic, but as life goes on you can learn from your experiences and develop a better understanding of yourself and the world around you.

You have a fondness for travel, appreciate beauty and harmony and hate disorder and strife. You may be fond of literature and would make a good writer or speaker yourself. You have a creative imagination and may come across as an incurable romantic. You have strong intuition, maybe bordering on a mediumistic quality, which sets you apart from the mass. You may not be rich in cash terms, but your personal gifts are worth more than gold.

PISCES IN LOVE

Discover how compatible in love you are with people from the same and other signs of the zodiac. Five stars equals a match made in heaven!

Pisces meets Pisces

Pisceans are easy-going and get on well with most people, so when two Pisceans get together, harmony is invariably the result. While this isn't the most dynamic relationship, there is mutual understanding, and a desire to please on both sides. Neither partner is likely to be overbearing or selfish. Family responsibilities should be happily shared and home surroundings will be comfortable, but never pretentious. One of the better pairings for the sign of the Fishes. Star rating: *****

Pisces meets Aries

Still waters run deep, and they don't come much deeper than Pisces. Although these signs share the same quadrant of the zodiac, they have little in common. Pisces is a dreamer, a romantic idealist with steady and spiritual goals. Aries needs to be on the move, and has very different ideals. It's hard to see how a relationship could develop but, with patience, there is a chance that things might work out. Pisces needs incentive, and Aries may be the sign to offer it. Star rating: **

Pisces meets Taurus

No problem here, unless both parties come from the quieter side of their respective signs. Most of the time Taurus and Pisces would live comfortably together, offering mutual support and deep regard. Taurus can offer the personal qualities that Pisces craves, whilst Pisces understands and copes with the Bull's slightly stubborn qualities. Taurus is likely to travel in Piscean company, so there is a potential for wide-ranging experiences and variety which is essential. There will be some misunderstandings, mainly because Pisces is so deep, but that won't prevent their enduring happiness. Star rating: ***

Pisces meets Gemini

Gemini likes to think of itself as intuitive and intellectual, but it will never understand Pisces' dark depths. Another stumbling block is that both Gemini and Pisces are 'split' signs – the Twins and the two Fishes – which means that both are capable of dual personalities. There won't be any shortage of affection, but the real question has to be how much these people feel they have in common. Pisces is extremely kind, and so is Gemini most of the time. But Pisces does too much soul-searching for Gemini, who might eventually become bored. Star rating: ***

Pisces meets Cancer

This is likely to be a very successful match. Cancer and Pisces are both Water signs, both deep, sensitive and very caring. Pisces loves deeply, and Cancer wants to be loved. There will be few fireworks here, and a very quiet house. But that doesn't mean that either love or action is lacking – the latter of which is just behind closed doors. Family and children are important to both signs and both are prepared to work hard, but Pisces is the more restless of the two and needs the support and security that Cancer offers. Star rating: *****

Pisces meets Leo

Pisces always needs to understand others, which makes Leo feel warm and loved, while Leo sees, to its delight, that Pisces needs to be protected and taken care of. Pisceans are often lacking in self-confidence which is something Leo has to spare, and happily it is often infectious. Pisces' inevitable cares are swept away on a tide of Leonine cheerfulness. This couple's home would be cheerful and full of love, which is beneficial to all family members. This is not a meeting of minds, but rather an understanding and appreciation of differences. Star rating: ****

Pisces meets Virgo

This looks an unpromising match from beginning to end. There are exceptions to every rule, particularly where Pisces is concerned, but these two signs are both so deep it's hard to imagine that they could ever find what makes the other tick. The depth is different in each case: Virgo's ruminations are extremely materialistic, while Pisces exists in a world of deep-felt, poorly expressed emotion. Pisces and Virgo might find they don't talk much, so only in a contemplative, almost monastic, match would they ever get on. Still, in a vast zodiac, anything is possible. Star rating: **

Pisces meets Libra

Libra and Pisces can be extremely fond of each other, even deeply in love, but this alone isn't a stable foundation for long-term success. Pisces is extremely deep and doesn't even know itself very well. Libra may initially find this intriguing but will eventually feel frustrated at being unable to understand the Piscean's emotional and personal feelings. Pisces can be jealous and may find Libra's flightiness difficult, which Libra can't stand. They are great friends and they may make it to the romantic stakes, but when they get there a great deal of effort will be necessary. Star rating: ***

Pisces meets Scorpio

If ever there were two zodiac signs that have a total rapport, it has to be Scorpio and Pisces. They share very similar needs: they are not gregarious and are happy with a little silence, good music and time to contemplate the finer things in life, and both are attracted to family life. Apart, they can have a tendency to wander in a romantic sense, but this is reduced when they come together. They are deep, firm friends who enjoy each other's company and this must lead to an excellent chance of success. These people are surely made for each other! Star rating: *****

Pisces meets Sagittarius

Probably the least likely success story for either sign, which is why it scores so low on the star rating. The basic problem is an almost total lack of understanding. A successful relationship needs empathy and progress towards a shared goal but, although both are eager to please, Pisces is too deep and Sagittarius too flighty – they just don't belong on the same planet! As pals, they have more in common and so a friendship is the best hope of success and happiness. Star rating: *

Pisces meets Capricorn

There is some chance of a happy relationship here, but it will need work on both sides. Capricorn is a go-getter, but likes to plan long term. Pisces is naturally more immediate, but has enough intuition to understand the Goat's thinking. Both have patience, but it will usually be Pisces who chooses to play second fiddle. The quiet nature of both signs might be a problem, as someone will have to take the lead, especially in social situations. Both signs should recognise this fact and accommodate it. Star rating: ***

Pisces meets Aquarius

Zodiac signs that follow each other often have something in common, but this is often not the case with Aquarius and Pisces. Both signs are deeply caring, but in different ways. Pisces is one of the deepest zodiac signs, and Aquarius simply isn't prepared to embark on the journey. Pisceans, meanwhile, would probably find Aquarians superficial and even flippant. On the positive side, there is potential for a well-balanced relationship, but unless one party is untypical of their zodiac sign, it often doesn't get started. Star rating: **

VENUS:
THE PLANET OF LOVE

If you look up at the sky around sunset or sunrise you will often see Venus in close attendance to the Sun. It is arguably one of the most beautiful sights of all and there is little wonder that historically it became associated with the goddess of love. But although Venus does play an important part in the way you view love and in the way others see you romantically, this is only one of the spheres of influence that it enjoys in your overall character.

Venus has a part to play in the more cultured side of your life and has much to do with your appreciation of art, literature, music and general creativity. Even the way you look is responsive to the part of the zodiac that Venus occupied at the start of your life, though this fact is also down to your Sun sign and Ascending sign. If, at the time you were born, Venus occupied one of the more gregarious zodiac signs, you will be more likely to wear your heart on your sleeve, as well as to be more attracted to entertainment, social gatherings and good company. If on the other hand Venus occupied a quiet zodiac sign at the time of your birth, you would tend to be more retiring and less willing to shine in public situations.

It's good to know what part the planet Venus plays in your life, for it can have a great bearing on the way you appear to the rest of the world and since we all have to mix with others, you can learn to make the very best of what Venus has to offer you.

One of the great complications in the past has always been trying to establish exactly what zodiac position Venus enjoyed when you were born, because the planet is notoriously difficult to track. However, I have solved that problem by creating a table that is exclusive to your Sun sign, which you will find on the following page.

Establishing your Venus sign could not be easier. Just look up the year of your birth on the page opposite and you will see a sign of the zodiac. This was the sign that Venus occupied in the period covered by your sign in that year. If Venus occupied more than one sign during the period, this is indicated by the date on which the sign changed, and the name of the new sign. For instance, if you were born in 1940, Venus was in Aries until the 9th March, after which time it was in Taurus. If you were born before 9th March your Venus sign is Aries, if you were born on or after 9th March, your Venus sign is Taurus. Once you have established the position of Venus at the time of your birth, you can then look in the pages which follow to see how this has a bearing on your life as a whole.

1919 PISCES / 27.2 ARIES
1920 CAPRICORN /
    24.2 AQUARIUS / 19.3 PISCES
1921 ARIES / 8.3 TAURUS
1922 PISCES / 14.3 ARIES
1923 CAPRICORN
1924 ARIES / 10.3 TAURUS
1925 AQUARIUS / 4.3 PISCES
1926 AQUARIUS
1927 PISCES / 26.2 ARIES
1928 CAPRICORN /
    23.2 AQUARIUS / 18.3 PISCES
1929 ARIES / 9.3 TAURUS
1930 PISCES / 13.3 ARIES
1931 CAPRICORN
1932 ARIES / 9.3 TAURUS
1933 AQUARIUS / 4.3 PISCES
1934 AQUARIUS
1935 PISCES / 25.2 ARIES
1936 CAPRICORN /
    23.2 AQUARIUS / 18.3 PISCES
1937 ARIES / 10.3 TAURUS
1938 PISCES / 12.3 ARIES
1939 CAPRICORN
1940 ARIES / 9.3 TAURUS
1941 AQUARIUS / 3.3 PISCES
1942 AQUARIUS
1943 PISCES / 25.2 ARIES
1944 CAPRICORN /
    22.2 AQUARIUS / 18.3 PISCES
1945 ARIES / 11.3 TAURUS
1946 PISCES / 11.3 ARIES
1947 CAPRICORN
1948 ARIES / 8.3 TAURUS
1949 AQUARIUS / 3.3 PISCES
1950 AQUARIUS
1951 PISCES / 24.2 ARIES
1952 CAPRICORN /
    22.2 AQUARIUS / 17.3 PISCES
1953 ARIES
1954 PISCES / 11.3 ARIES
1955 CAPRICORN
1956 ARIES / 8.3 TAURUS
1957 AQUARIUS / 2.3 PISCES
1958 CAPRICORN /
    25.2 AQUARIUS
1959 PISCES / 24.2 ARIES
1960 CAPRICORN /
    21.2 AQUARIUS / 17.3 PISCES
1961 ARIES
1962 PISCES / 10.3 ARIES
1963 CAPRICORN
1964 ARIES / 8.3 TAURUS
1965 AQUARIUS / 1.3 PISCES
1966 AQUARIUS
1967 PISCES / 23.2 ARIES
1968 SAGITTARIUS /
    26.1 CAPRICORN

1969 ARIES
1970 PISCES / 10.3 ARIES
1971 CAPRICORN
1972 ARIES / 7.3 TAURUS
1973 AQUARIUS / 1.3 PISCES
1974 CAPRICORN / 2.3 AQUARIUS
1975 PISCES / 23.2 ARIES
1976 SAGITTARIUS /
    26.1 CAPRICORN
1977 ARIES
1978 PISCES / 9.3 ARIES
1979 CAPRICORN
1980 ARIES / 7.3 TAURUS
1981 AQUARIUS / 28.2 PISCES
1982 CAPRICORN / 4.3 AQUARIUS
1983 PISCES / 23.2 ARIES
1984 SAGITTARIUS /
    25.1 CAPRICORN
1985 ARIES
1986 PISCES / 9.3 ARIES
1987 CAPRICORN
1988 ARIES / 7.3 TAURUS
1989 AQUARIUS / 28.2 PISCES
1990 CAPRICORN / 5.3 AQUARIUS
1991 PISCES / 22.2 ARIES /
    20.3 TAURUS
1992 SAGITTARIUS /
    25.1 CAPRICORN
1993 ARIES
1994 PISCES / 9.3 ARIES
1995 CAPRICORN
1996 ARIES / 7.3 TAURUS
1997 AQUARIUS / 27.2 PISCES
1998 CAPRICORN / 5.3 AQUARIUS
1999 PISCES / 22.2 ARIES /
    19.3 TAURUS
2000 SAGITTARIUS /
    25.1 CAPRICORN
2001 ARIES
2002 PISCES / 9.3 ARIES
2003 CAPRICORN
2004 ARIES / 7.3 TAURUS
2005 AQUARIUS / 27.2 PISCES
2006 CAPRICORN / 5.3 AQUARIUS
2007 PISCES / 22.2 ARIES
2008 SAGITTARIUS /
    25.1 CAPRICORN
2009 ARIES
2010 PISCES / 9.3 ARIES
2011 CAPRICORN
2012 ARIES / 7.3 TAURUS
2013 AQUARIUS / 27.2 PISCES
2014 AQUARIUS / 27.2 PISCES
2015 PISCES / 22.2 ARIES
2016 AQUARIUS / 6.2 PISCES
2017 ARIES

VENUS THROUGH THE ZODIAC SIGNS

Venus in Aries

Amongst other things, the position of Venus in Aries indicates a fondness for travel, music and all creative pursuits. Your nature tends to be affectionate and you would try not to create confusion or difficulty for others if it could be avoided. Many people with this planetary position have a great love of the theatre, and mental stimulation is of the greatest importance. Early romantic attachments are common with Venus in Aries, so it is very important to establish a genuine sense of romantic continuity. Early marriage is not recommended, especially if it is based on sympathy. You may give your heart a little too readily on occasions.

Venus in Taurus

You are capable of very deep feelings and your emotions tend to last for a very long time. This makes you a trusting partner and lover, whose constancy is second to none. In life you are precise and careful and always try to do things the right way. Although this means an ordered life, which you are comfortable with, it can also lead you to be rather too fussy for your own good. Despite your pleasant nature, you are very fixed in your opinions and quite able to speak your mind. Others are attracted to you and historical astrologers always quoted this position of Venus as being very fortunate in terms of marriage. However, if you find yourself involved in a failed relationship, it could take you a long time to trust again.

Venus in Gemini

As with all associations related to Gemini, you tend to be quite versatile, anxious for change and intelligent in your dealings with the world at large. You may gain money from more than one source but you are equally good at spending it. There is an inference here that you are a good communicator, via either the written or the spoken word, and you love to be in the company of interesting people. Always on the look-out for culture, you may also be very fond of music, and love to indulge the curious and cultured side of your nature. In romance you tend to have more than one relationship and could find yourself associated with someone who has previously been a friend or even a distant relative.

Venus in Cancer

You often stay close to home because you are very fond of family and enjoy many of your most treasured moments when you are with those you love. Being naturally sympathetic, you will always do anything you can to support those around you, even people you hardly know at all. This charitable side of your nature is your most noticeable trait and is one of the reasons why others are naturally so fond of you. Being receptive and in some cases even psychic, you can see through to the soul of most of those with whom you come into contact. You may not commence too many romantic attachments but when you do give your heart, it tends to be unconditionally.

Venus in Leo

It must become quickly obvious to almost anyone you meet that you are kind, sympathetic and yet determined enough to stand up for anyone or anything that is truly important to you. Bright and sunny, you warm the world with your natural enthusiasm and would rarely do anything to hurt those around you, or at least not intentionally. In romance you are ardent and sincere, though some may find your style just a little overpowering. Gains come through your contacts with other people and this could be especially true with regard to romance, for love and money often come hand in hand for those who were born with Venus in Leo. People claim to understand you, though you are more complex than you seem.

Venus in Virgo

Your nature could well be fairly quiet no matter what your Sun sign might be, though this fact often manifests itself as an inner peace and would not prevent you from being basically sociable. Some delays and even the odd disappointment in love cannot be ruled out with this planetary position, though it's a fact that you will usually find the happiness you look for in the end. Catapulting yourself into romantic entanglements that you know to be rather ill-advised is not sensible, and it would be better to wait before you committed yourself exclusively to any one person. It is the essence of your nature to serve the world at large and through doing so it is possible that you will attract money at some stage in your life.

Venus in Libra

Venus is very comfortable in Libra and bestows upon those people who have this planetary position a particular sort of kindness that is easy to recognise. This is a very good position for all sorts of friendships and also for romantic attachments that usually bring much joy into your life. Few individuals with Venus in Libra would avoid marriage and since you are capable of great depths of love, it is likely that you will find a contented personal life. You like to mix with people of integrity and intelligence but don't take kindly to scruffy surroundings or work that means getting your hands too dirty. Careful speculation, good business dealings and money through marriage all seem fairly likely.

Venus in Scorpio

You are quite open and tend to spend money quite freely, even on those occasions when you don't have very much. Although your intentions are always good, there are times when you get yourself in to the odd scrape and this can be particularly true when it comes to romance, which you may come to late or from a rather unexpected direction. Certainly you have the power to be happy and to make others contented on the way, but you find the odd stumbling block on your journey through life and it could seem that you have to work harder than those around you. As a result of this, you gain a much deeper understanding of the true value of personal happiness than many people ever do, and are likely to achieve true contentment in the end.

Venus in Sagittarius

You are lighthearted, cheerful and always able to see the funny side of any situation. These facts enhance your popularity, which is especially high with members of the opposite sex. You should never have to look too far to find romantic interest in your life, though it is just possible that you might be too willing to commit yourself before you are certain that the person in question is right for you. Part of the problem here extends to other areas of life too. The fact is that you like variety in everything and so can tire of situations that fail to offer it. All the same, if you choose wisely and learn to understand your restless side, then great happiness can be yours.

Venus in Capricorn

The most notable trait that comes from Venus in this position is that it makes you trustworthy and able to take on all sorts of responsibilities in life. People are instinctively fond of you and love you all the more because you are always ready to help those who are in any form of need. Social and business popularity can be yours and there is a magnetic quality to your nature that is particularly attractive in a romantic sense. Anyone who wants a partner for a lover, a spouse and a good friend too would almost certainly look in your direction. Constancy is the hallmark of your nature and unfaithfulness would go right against the grain. You might sometimes be a little too trusting.

Venus in Aquarius

This location of Venus offers a fondness for travel and a desire to try out something new at every possible opportunity. You are extremely easy to get along with and tend to have many friends from varied backgrounds, classes and inclinations. You like to live a distinct sort of life and gain a great deal from moving about, both in a career sense and with regard to your home. It is not out of the question that you could form a romantic attachment to someone who comes from far away or be attracted to a person of a distinctly artistic and original nature. What you cannot stand is jealousy, for you have friends of both sexes and would want to keep things that way.

Venus in Pisces

The first thing people tend to notice about you is your wonderful, warm smile. Being very charitable by nature you will do anything to help others, even if you don't know them well. Much of your life may be spent sorting out situations for other people, but it is very important to feel that you are living for yourself too. In the main, you remain cheerful, and tend to be quite attractive to members of the opposite sex. Where romantic attachments are concerned, you could be drawn to people who are significantly older or younger than yourself or to someone with a unique career or point of view. It might be best for you to avoid marrying whilst you are still very young.

HOW THE DIAGRAMS WORK

Through the picture diagrams in the Astral Diary I want to help you to plot your year. With them you can see where the positive and negative aspects will be found in each month. To make the most of them, all you have to do is remember where and when!

Let me show you how they work ...

THE MONTH AT A GLANCE

Just as there are twelve separate zodiac signs, so astrologers believe that each sign has twelve separate aspects to life. Each of the twelve segments relates to a different personal aspect. I list them all every month so that their meanings are always clear.

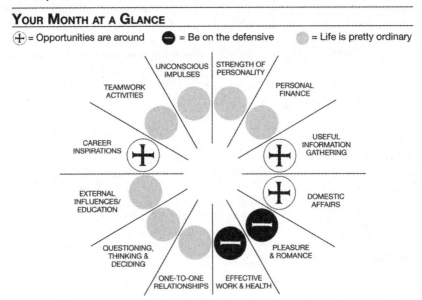

YOUR MONTH AT A GLANCE

⊕ = Opportunities are around ● = Be on the defensive ◐ = Life is pretty ordinary

UNCONSCIOUS IMPULSES
STRENGTH OF PERSONALITY
TEAMWORK ACTIVITIES
PERSONAL FINANCE
CAREER INSPIRATIONS
USEFUL INFORMATION GATHERING
EXTERNAL INFLUENCES/ EDUCATION
DOMESTIC AFFAIRS
QUESTIONING, THINKING & DECIDING
PLEASURE & ROMANCE
ONE-TO-ONE RELATIONSHIPS
EFFECTIVE WORK & HEALTH

I have designed this chart to show you how and when these twelve different aspects are being influenced throughout the year. When there is a shaded circle, nothing out of the ordinary is to be expected. However, when a circle turns white with a plus sign, the influence is positive. Where the circle is black with a minus sign, it is a negative.

YOUR ENERGY RHYTHM CHART

Below is a picture diagram in which I link your zodiac group to the rhythm of the Moon. In doing this I have calculated when you will be gaining strength from its influence and equally when you may be weakened by it.

If you think of yourself as being like the tides of the ocean then you may understand how your own energies must also rise and fall. And if you understand how it works and when it is working, then you can better organise your activities to achieve more and get things done more easily.

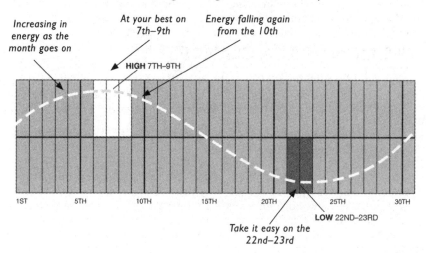

THE KEY DAYS

Some of the entries are in **bold**, which indicates the working of astrological cycles in your life. Look out for them each week as they are the best days to take action or make decisions. The daily text tells you which area of your life to focus on.

MERCURY RETROGRADE

The Mercury symbol (☿) indicates that Mercury is retrograde on that day. Since Mercury governs communication, the fact that it appears to be moving backwards when viewed from the Earth at this time should warn you that your communication skills are not likely to be at their best and you could expect some setbacks.

PISCES: YOUR YEAR IN BRIEF

Perhaps uncommonly for Pisces, you look towards a new year with great optimism and a degree of excitement. January and February should not let you down because both months are likely to be dynamic and enterprising. Don't be fooled into thinking that other people know better than you do because the chances are that they don't. Take the line of least resistance when dealing with romantic matters and things should go smoothly.

It appears that March and April should find you feeling fairly relaxed and able to settle into situations to a greater extent than at the beginning of the year. You know what you want, especially from personal attachments, and romance ought to play an important part in your life. April will probably bring a period of intensive spring-cleaning to every area in which you are involved.

During May and June you display yourself in the best possible light and should be gaining new friends and allies as a result. You are confident to do the right thing at work, but you can expect some upheaval at home unless you pay it more attention. The trouble is that not everyone around you is inspired by the same plans and ideas that you are.

Traditionally speaking, July and August are the hottest months and should prove to be so in more ways than one as far as Pisces is concerned. It is at this time that personal relationships are heating up no end and when romance is probably the most important part of your life. There may be a renewed commitment to an old task and also a chance for you to get in touch with people you haven't seen for ages. Almost everyone you know seems to be working for your advancement during this interlude.

As is often the case for Pisces, September and October bring a need for greater domestic security and a tendency to stick closer to home. This does not mean an end to your progressive attitude or to your travels. It merely infers that your nearest and dearest will be the most important part of your life and that you might be just slightly more timid than previously. This is not especially unusual for the zodiac sign of Pisces.

It is important – and also relevant – to have confidence in yourself at the very end of the year and to trust your instinctive sense of what will work out well. Romance certainly continues to be very well highlighted at this time and you should be energetic and progressive during both November and December. Christmas should offer you a great deal more than you might have expected, both in terms of surprises and upward turns in relationships. The lunar high coincides with Christmas itself – which is a rare and fortunate treat.

January 2017

Your Month at a Glance

$\oplus$ = Opportunities are around   ⊖ = Be on the defensive   ⬤ = Life is pretty ordinary

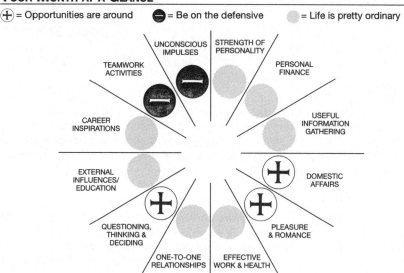

STRENGTH OF
PERSONALITY

UNCONSCIOUS
IMPULSES

PERSONAL
FINANCE

TEAMWORK
ACTIVITIES

USEFUL
INFORMATION
GATHERING

CAREER
INSPIRATIONS

DOMESTIC
AFFAIRS

EXTERNAL
INFLUENCES/
EDUCATION

PLEASURE
& ROMANCE

QUESTIONING,
THINKING &
DECIDING

ONE-TO-ONE
RELATIONSHIPS

EFFECTIVE
WORK & HEALTH

January Highs and Lows

Here I show you how the rhythms of the Moon will affect you this month. Like the tide, your energies and abilities will rise and fall with its pattern. When it is above the centre line, go for it, when it is below, you should be resting.

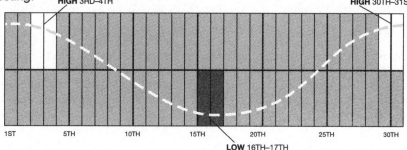

HIGH 3RD–4TH

HIGH 30TH–31ST

1ST   5TH   10TH   15TH   20TH   25TH   30TH

LOW 16TH–17TH

1 SUNDAY ☿ *Moon Age Day 4   Moon Sign Aquarius*

If you insist on confiding in others on this New Year's Day you might end up somewhat disappointed. Not everyone will prove to be either as reliable or as secretive as you would like them to be. All in all, this trend could make you suspicious but your intuition is good and if you listen to it you will know who to trust.

2 MONDAY ☿ *Moon Age Day 5   Moon Sign Aquarius*

Intimate relationships could now prove to be slightly more demanding than of late. Family members might also ask a great deal of you, but happily there is no indication that you will let them down. Just remember that you will also need some time to yourself and that you are entitled to consideration too.

3 TUESDAY ☿ *Moon Age Day 6   Moon Sign Pisces*

The Moon enters your zodiac sign, bringing one of the most productive and generally lucky periods of the month. Whatever you take on today, go for gold. Don't be shy of letting people know you are around and show even those people who think they know you well that there is more to you than meets the eye.

4 WEDNESDAY ☿ *Moon Age Day 7   Moon Sign Pisces*

There is little time to rest at the moment but this won't worry you much at all. You are at your best when out and about and you certainly would not take kindly to being cooped up in the same place all day. Good luck is on your side and might bring a few surprises by the latter part of the day.

5 THURSDAY ☿ *Moon Age Day 8   Moon Sign Aries*

You have plenty of energy today and may decide that an outing or a shopping spree would suit you down to the ground. Spend time with family members or friends and also make the most of romantic opportunities. If you have specifically been looking for love, now is the time to focus your attention.

6 FRIDAY ☿ *Moon Age Day 9   Moon Sign Aries*

You are a sucker today for anyone who has the gift of the gab. That's fine but don't allow yourself to be duped by anyone simply because they spin a good yarn. Trends suggest that this would not be an ideal day for making major purchases or for doing anything that relies on instinctive decisions instead of rational thought.

7 SATURDAY ☿   *Moon Age Day 10   Moon Sign Taurus*

If you find one or two mishaps coming along today, don't panic. Either start again at the beginning or seek the help and advice of someone who is a professional in their field. Don't be in the least surprised if you turn out to be someone's particular cup of tea because it looks like your popularity is now on the rise.

8 SUNDAY   *Moon Age Day 11   Moon Sign Taurus*

It doesn't matter how much you rehearse, there are things to do in the week ahead that you may be dreading. Most likely this is because you are going to have to be in the public eye. Don't let thoughts about this spoil your Sunday. The stars show how well you are going to cope with anything between now and next weekend.

9 MONDAY   *Moon Age Day 12   Moon Sign Gemini*

This is not a day to believe everything you hear. Although there may be nobody deliberately pulling the wool over your eyes, that's the way it might seem. Analyse situations carefully and only act when you know you have thought things through very carefully. Friends should prove to be generally reliable.

10 TUESDAY   *Moon Age Day 13   Moon Sign Gemini*

The planetary positions in your chart incline you to think everything through carefully now. You are fairly sociable but may be inclined to withdraw from large groups of people or situations that put you in the spotlight. Look after money carefully today and only spend when you know you are getting a bargain.

11 WEDNESDAY   *Moon Age Day 14   Moon Sign Cancer*

A period of significant financial gain could be coming along now. Ideas you had in the past are likely to mature. Avoid worrying too much about situations you can't control and make certain you feather your own nest, as well as those of everyone you know. This is about as selfish as Pisces ever gets so make the most of it.

12 THURSDAY   *Moon Age Day 15   Moon Sign Cancer*

You should feel well in tune with life now, thanks in part to the efforts of friends, many of whom seem to be doing all they can to please you at this time. The welfare of other people is always close to the Piscean heart and trends suggest that you could be taking on some challenges soon in the name of charity.

13 FRIDAY
Moon Age Day 16   Moon Sign Cancer

You should enjoy good conversation today and can also find your romantic world looking very bright. By the evening you will probably be feeling very much like an outing and could well be with friends. Someone you counted as only an acquaintance is likely to be joining your circle of friends before very long.

14 SATURDAY
Moon Age Day 17   Moon Sign Leo

The pace of life is likely to be brisk now and there is no shortage of things you want to get done. Look out for some very positive compliments coming your way. You might not exactly believe them but the fact that they are there at all is inclined to make you feel better about life generally.

15 SUNDAY
Moon Age Day 18   Moon Sign Leo

Your ability to win friends and to influence people is noteworthy today and you should not avoid any opportunity that comes along to feather your own nest. Your confidence remains essentially high and the slightly retiring qualities inherent in the sign of Pisces don't seem to be on display now.

16 MONDAY
Moon Age Day 19   Moon Sign Virgo

This is the first lunar low of the year. This is the time each month during which the Moon occupies your opposite sign of Virgo. You might feel slightly under the weather, or simply inclined to spend some time on your own. This is not the best day of the month for taking chances, but rather for taking it easy.

17 TUESDAY
Moon Age Day 20   Moon Sign Virgo

The working week is well underway for many Pisceans but under the continuing influence of the lunar low you may not be inclined to get involved in anything complicated. This is a good day for planning but less useful for taking action. If you can force yourself to take a broad overview of life, so much the better.

18 WEDNESDAY
Moon Age Day 21   Moon Sign Libra

You are now in a good position to overcome a few reversals that might have been around since late last year. This is particularly true at work, where you seem to be making a good impression on others. If you are ahead of yourself with certain tasks you ought to be willing to take some time out to focus on something else.

19 THURSDAY
Moon Age Day 22   Moon Sign Libra

Look for a change of scenery if you really want to keep smiling today. You won't be at all happy with being kept in the same place and diversity is what really fires off your imagination at this time. Mental and intellectual matters are uppermost and you would be incredible at solving puzzles or brainteasers now.

20 FRIDAY
Moon Age Day 23   Moon Sign Scorpio

You might have to learn to use a little more concentration when it comes to assessing the needs of those around you. This is a strange statement to make to anyone born under the zodiac sign of Pisces, which is the most caring sign of them all. However, for today the position of the Moon is doing you few favours in this regard.

21 SATURDAY
Moon Age Day 24   Moon Sign Scorpio

Information coming your way from a friend or associate could do much to brighten your weekend. Your state of mind generally can be improved as a result of social possibilities that are coming your way now. Romance cannot be ruled out as being an important component to this weekend.

22 SUNDAY
Moon Age Day 25   Moon Sign Scorpio

It is possible that practical or professional responsibilities could increase at this time, thanks to the position of the planet Mars in your solar chart. Other planetary positions give you the resilience and strength you are going to need to make the most what the most forceful planet of them all is offering.

23 MONDAY
Moon Age Day 26   Moon Sign Sagittarius

There is much to keep you happy, busy and on the go now. You probably will not have the time to think about things too deeply and that could be a major factor in some of your successes. You are thinking on your feet and that has to be positive when it comes to scoring personal successes.

24 TUESDAY
Moon Age Day 27   Moon Sign Sagittarius

New input should be welcomed with open arms at this time. This is a great period for making new contacts, whether these are people you seek for yourself or not. Everyone seems to want to be your friend at the moment and there is no reason to feel quite as nervous about situations as you sometimes do.

25 WEDNESDAY
Moon Age Day 28   Moon Sign Capricorn

There are now exciting social possibilities to look at, though not for long because today really depends on acting quickly. You can have a really good time in the company of people who have a very casual attitude to life. Sometimes this is good for a person who is generally a very deep thinker and brings a little light relief.

26 THURSDAY
Moon Age Day 29   Moon Sign Capricorn

Avoid unnecessary assumptions and bear in mind that you could be rather susceptible to deceptions and hidden schemes around now. This would not be a good time to sign any documents unless you are certain of the small print. Confidences from friends need to be kept strictly to yourself at this time.

27 FRIDAY
Moon Age Day 0   Moon Sign Capricorn

You really do need to get your act together in a professional sense if you want to take full advantage of an offer that is about to come your way. It is possible that you will doubt yourself, which is a pity because you seem to be on top form and can easily excel in situations that puzzle those around you.

28 SATURDAY
Moon Age Day 1   Moon Sign Aquarius

Social invitations are likely to come thick and fast now and they bring with them the chance to really enjoy what the weekend, and Saturday in particular, has to offer. If you have been looking for love it is quite possible you will find it under present trends. Don't give in if there is something you really want but go out on a limb to get it.

29 SUNDAY
Moon Age Day 2   Moon Sign Aquarius

Don't believe everything you hear from others at the moment and then you won't be too disappointed when things don't go the way you might have wished. You are likely to have a reserve strategy under all circumstances now and this would be wise. Confronting an old dragon is possible for some of you now.

30 MONDAY
Moon Age Day 3   Moon Sign Pisces

The lunar high brings many favours and high-spots into your life. When it comes to making fresh starts you could hardly be doing better and all the planning you have been doing now begins to pay off. You can expect a boost to your life in both a professional and a social sense and the difference really shows.

31 TUESDAY
Moon Age Day 4   Moon Sign Pisces

Now your personal horizons will broaden immeasurably. You believe in yourself and that's worth so much. Romantic matters are particularly well highlighted, not only by the lunar high but also by the position of Venus in your chart. In a practical or a professional sense it is very important to strike while the iron is hot.

February

2017

YOUR MONTH AT A GLANCE

⊕ = Opportunities are around   ⊖ = Be on the defensive   ⬤ = Life is pretty ordinary

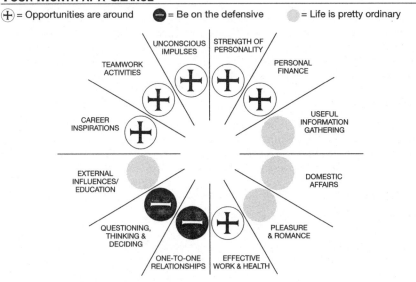

UNCONSCIOUS IMPULSES

STRENGTH OF PERSONALITY

TEAMWORK ACTIVITIES

PERSONAL FINANCE

CAREER INSPIRATIONS

USEFUL INFORMATION GATHERING

EXTERNAL INFLUENCES/ EDUCATION

DOMESTIC AFFAIRS

QUESTIONING, THINKING & DECIDING

PLEASURE & ROMANCE

ONE-TO-ONE RELATIONSHIPS

EFFECTIVE WORK & HEALTH

FEBRUARY HIGHS AND LOWS

Here I show you how the rhythms of the Moon will affect you this month. Like the tide, your energies and abilities will rise and fall with its pattern. When it is above the centre line, go for it, when it is below, you should be resting.

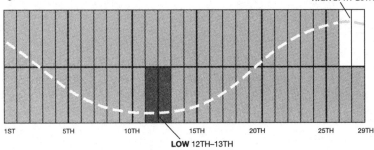

HIGH 27TH–28TH

1ST   5TH   10TH   15TH   20TH   25TH   29TH

LOW 12TH–13TH

1 WEDNESDAY
Moon Age Day 5   Moon Sign Aries

You could find yourself hanging back if you think that too much is being expected of you. This is a time to talk things through with others in a frank and honest way and to put forward your usual rational point of view. Your confidence should be reasonably high, especially if you are dealing with projects you understand.

2 THURSDAY
Moon Age Day 6   Moon Sign Aries

You are keeping a higher profile today and may find yourself mixing with some very interesting types. There are career moves in the offing for some Pisceans, though you might turn an offer down if you feel it isn't going in the direction you would wish. Keep an eye open for some quite amazing possibilities socially.

3 FRIDAY
Moon Age Day 7   Moon Sign Aries

It is quite likely you will be thinking about personal issues today and perhaps seeking to change the ground rules with regard to a relationship. People you haven't seen for some time could be returning to your life soon, and trends suggest that they may bring with them some surprising news.

4 SATURDAY
Moon Age Day 8   Moon Sign Taurus

When it comes to dealing with others, there are now a few obstacles to deal with. Not everyone is behaving in quite the way you would expect and you are perhaps a little touchy at present. There could be occasions today when you will need to exercise that famous Piscean patience, though it won't be easy.

5 SUNDAY
Moon Age Day 9   Moon Sign Taurus

This should be a positive period on the domestic scene. It looks as though you are in for some interesting times with regard to family members, with younger people figuring strongly in your life. Although you won't consider yourself to be particularly lucky at the moment, there are some gains possible.

6 MONDAY
Moon Age Day 10   Moon Sign Gemini

You are especially sensitive to the feelings of those around you as this new week gets underway. Although you want to please everyone, this won't be possible and it will almost certainly be necessary for you to speak your mind at some stage. Where finances are concerned, hold on tight to money for the moment.

7 TUESDAY
Moon Age Day 11   Moon Sign Gemini

Recent small successes could be greatly improved upon, just as long as you concentrate and don't allow others to make either the running or the decisions. You are very astute at present and you have a strong instinct for what is the right action in any given situation. As a result, your level of confidence grows.

8 WEDNESDAY
Moon Age Day 12   Moon Sign Cancer

You should enjoy the cut and thrust of relationships immensely during the middle of this week and can gain a great deal simply from being around people you recognise as being successful in their own right. You might detect a small but steadily growing desire to break out of some social or personal constraints.

9 THURSDAY
Moon Age Day 13   Moon Sign Cancer

It may be necessary to take a more commanding role in your family than you are used to and this could turn out to be a very good thing. Although it could seem to you that you are lording it over others, nothing could be further from the truth. Partnerships of all sorts are well highlighted under present planetary trends.

10 FRIDAY
Moon Age Day 14   Moon Sign Leo

You won't lack stamina now and can achieve a good deal simply by bulldozing your way through situations. Maybe you will not show the same degree of sensitivity as is usually the case but you can make rapid progress in a number of different spheres. If your memory lets you down it is probably because you are overloading it.

11 SATURDAY
Moon Age Day 15   Moon Sign Leo

There are some jobs this weekend that are going to seem more trouble than they are worth. The reason for this is simple. You want to have fun and won't take at all kindly to being held back by anyone or anything. You should find the ability to take decisive action, even though you might wonder where it came from.

12 SUNDAY
Moon Age Day 16   Moon Sign Virgo

Things could slow down somewhat this Sunday for two reasons. Firstly, the lunar low is around and secondly, the sort of progress you have been making is tied to practical and professional matters. Although some impatience is very likely, take time to contemplate the quieter and more reflective side of your zodiac sign.

13 MONDAY
Moon Age Day 17   Moon Sign Virgo

This is a time to catch up with intimate relationships and to stay mainly in the bosom of your family. Nobody is forcing you down this road and, in any case, the temporary respite should prove to have been extremely useful, once tomorrow comes and the lunar low is out of the way.

14 TUESDAY
Moon Age Day 18   Moon Sign Libra

If there are any frustrations about today, they are likely to come about as a result of the activities of others. Unfortunately, you will have to take these in your stride because there is very little you can do about them. A mixture of loyalty and Piscean sensitivity will most likely prevent you from firing back.

15 WEDNESDAY
Moon Age Day 19   Moon Sign Libra

Moneymaking endeavours are well starred and continue to be so between now and the weekend. Although you won't want to take too many chances, you do have a sort of astrological guardian angel looking over you. When it comes to putting forward your unique point of view, tell it how it is.

16 THURSDAY
Moon Age Day 20   Moon Sign Libra

You are probably the best team player on the block at the moment and you won't go short of attention, either in a professional or a personal sense. People love to have you around and recognise you as a cheerful and positive person whose energy can lift their spirits. Simply enjoy what today has to offer.

17 FRIDAY
Moon Age Day 21   Moon Sign Scorpio

It is important to be clearer than ever when it comes to discussing matters with others. Don't leave any doubt whatsoever as to your point of view and ensure that everyone you come across knows the way you feel. That aside, there ought to be space and time to simply enjoy yourself at this stage of the week.

18 SATURDAY
Moon Age Day 22   Moon Sign Scorpio

The focus now is on communication. Talking to others as much as possible puts you in the picture with regard to practical and professional matters and ensures that you don't lose your way. Friends should prove to be especially helpful at the moment and have a greater than average desire to help you out.

19 SUNDAY
Moon Age Day 23   Moon Sign Sagittarius

You may be slightly uncomfortable in certain social situations today but there is no real reason for this except your own natural shyness. Once again, self-belief is the key to success and you should find that relatives and friends are offering the sort of compliments that makes it possible for you to be positive.

20 MONDAY
Moon Age Day 24   Moon Sign Sagittarius

Your most rewarding area of life now concerns domestic and family issues. This may prevent you from pushing as hard in the professional arena as you might wish but it is really only possible to concentrate completely on one thing at a time for now. Don't be too quick to blow a small family issue up into something serious.

21 TUESDAY
Moon Age Day 25   Moon Sign Sagittarius

You naturally gravitate towards positions of responsibility and power at this time. The Sun is just in your solar first house and is indicating that people will look at you first. You are attractive to others for a number of different reasons but you need to believe in yourself to complete the picture.

22 WEDNESDAY
Moon Age Day 26   Moon Sign Capricorn

Keep track of everything that is happening around you and be certain that you turn your intuition up to full when it comes to assessing the actions and reactions of others. This is particularly important if you have to sign any document or take on any long-term financial commitment. Make sure you are getting value for money.

23 THURSDAY
Moon Age Day 27   Moon Sign Capricorn

There might be emotional matters coming to the surface today that you would prefer to be left in the past. You could be right but on the other hand unless you settle them in your mind, they will simply come back to bother you time and again. This might be the day for a good heart-to-heart talk with your partner or a relative.

24 FRIDAY
Moon Age Day 28   Moon Sign Aquarius

At this time you could be pausing to enjoy some of the compliments that are likely to be coming in. However, don't preen yourself too much or you may lose sight of something important that has to be done today. Situations from the past have a habit of revisiting you in the present around now.

25 SATURDAY
Moon Age Day 0   Moon Sign Aquarius

There is plenty to keep you interested today, the only real problem being whether or not you have the time to fit in everything that takes your fancy. If a particular task or interest has been tiring you of late, leave it alone. Family members are likely to be calling upon you for assistance.

26 SUNDAY
Moon Age Day 1   Moon Sign Aquarius

What matters most about today is a generally improved situation in terms of the way you communicate. It should not be at all difficult to tell others exactly what you think now and since you are also very diplomatic, you can put your message across in a very positive and inspirational way.

27 MONDAY
Moon Age Day 2   Moon Sign Pisces

Professional objectives are the ones most supported by the lunar high this time around and you may decide the time is right to make a major change in a career sense. Although not every single person you come across seems to accept your point of view, those who don't are likely to be the exceptions rather than the rule.

28 TUESDAY
Moon Age Day 3   Moon Sign Pisces

Many aspects of your life should be looking brighter now. Good luck comes to you and might even catch you unawares in one or two respects. Although it isn't really like Pisces to chance its arm, you can afford just a little cautious flutter at the moment if you use your common sense and intuition and never gamble more than you can afford to lose.

March 2017

YOUR MONTH AT A GLANCE

$\oplus$ = Opportunities are around   ⚫ = Be on the defensive   ⚪ = Life is pretty ordinary

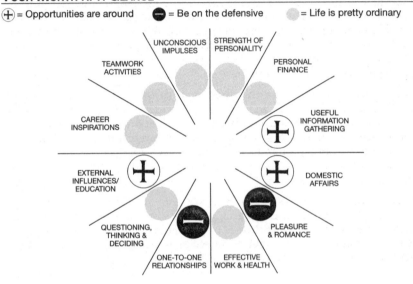

- UNCONSCIOUS IMPULSES
- STRENGTH OF PERSONALITY
- TEAMWORK ACTIVITIES
- PERSONAL FINANCE
- CAREER INSPIRATIONS
- USEFUL INFORMATION GATHERING
- EXTERNAL INFLUENCES/ EDUCATION
- DOMESTIC AFFAIRS
- QUESTIONING, THINKING & DECIDING
- PLEASURE & ROMANCE
- ONE-TO-ONE RELATIONSHIPS
- EFFECTIVE WORK & HEALTH

MARCH HIGHS AND LOWS

Here I show you how the rhythms of the Moon will affect you this month. Like the tide, your energies and abilities will rise and fall with its pattern. When it is above the centre line, go for it, when it is below, you should be resting.

HIGH 26TH–27TH

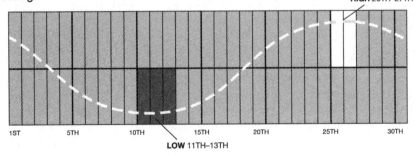

1ST   5TH   10TH   15TH   20TH   25TH   30TH

LOW 11TH–13TH

1 WEDNESDAY
Moon Age Day 4   Moon Sign Aries

Get your partner to open up if you suspect something is troubling them. There may be many confidences coming your way from other directions, too. A few of these might prove helpful to your own future but being born under the sign of Pisces, you are unlikely to betray a trust or sacrifice the well-being of others for your own gain.

2 THURSDAY
Moon Age Day 5   Moon Sign Aries

The planets suggest that you should have assistance on hand if you find yourself coming up against some sort of problem, even if you are a little too proud to ask for it. When life gets particularly tedious you may take comfort in daydreams, a useful respite for your sign on occasions. The evening should be good for social and romantic pursuits.

3 FRIDAY
Moon Age Day 6   Moon Sign Taurus

The year is moving on and it is possible that the weather is beginning to improve. As you may feel cooped up and uninspired if you stick around at home, how about a short trip? If you can get yourself out and into the company of people you find stimulating and interesting, then so much the better.

4 SATURDAY
Moon Age Day 7   Moon Sign Taurus

The responses you get from others at present are extremely promising, which is why this might turn out to be an excellent day for making suggestions. There are several areas of your life that could be improved with a little reorganisation. Now you have the chance to look at specifics and to deal with them.

5 SUNDAY
Moon Age Day 8   Moon Sign Gemini

There are possible gains to be made in your love life, perhaps because you are talking more and allowing your partner into the deepest recesses of that Piscean mind. In a business sense, new opportunities should be coming your way at any time now, bringing you closer to achieving some longed-for objectives.

6 MONDAY
Moon Age Day 9   Moon Sign Gemini

It looks as though pleasure is on the agenda as a new week commences. Although you are quite capable of working hard at this time, you should also be willing to take time out to simply enjoy yourself. On the way, you might be able to bring pleasure to those around you, especially family members.

7 TUESDAY
Moon Age Day 10   Moon Sign Cancer

Your natural curiosity comes to the fore very noticeably now. Anything and everything can capture your fertile imagination and nothing is outside your need to know. The only cautionary note is that you must make sure others don't think you are being nosey – even if, in fact, you are!

8 WEDNESDAY
Moon Age Day 11   Moon Sign Cancer

You are quick and efficient in all practical matters today, leaving those around you in no doubt whatsoever that you know what you are doing. In workplace situations, you will probably want to do your own thing and may not respond well if others have unrealistic expectations, no matter how nicely they are put to you.

9 THURSDAY
Moon Age Day 12   Moon Sign Leo

There are plenty of planetary influences about now that could lead to exciting social encounters. You are in a position to meet some interesting and influential people, both at work and in your social life. Expect some slight disagreements between yourself and family members or friends you know very well.

10 FRIDAY
Moon Age Day 13   Moon Sign Leo

The most competitive side of Pisces now begins to show. It doesn't matter whether you are thinking in terms of sport or even professional matters, the urge to win will be there. Your drive and determination power you on to go for gold, perhaps unusually for someone born under your zodiac sign.

11 SATURDAY
Moon Age Day 14   Moon Sign Virgo

Today's trends suggest that you need to keep to tried-and-tested paths for the moment, otherwise you might find difficulties starting to bubble up around you. The lunar low is likely to sap your strength somewhat and can certainly make it more difficult to assess the way others are likely to behave under any given circumstance.

12 SUNDAY
Moon Age Day 15   Moon Sign Virgo

Where practical logic is concerned, you might have to consult someone else right now. In some situations it could appear that you are walking blind into the heart of something you don't understand, and so you will need the assistance of people who know the way forward better than you do. Such trends are fleeting but they can be significant.

13 MONDAY
Moon Age Day 16   Moon Sign Virgo

You have a strong desire to help others and may prove time and again today that you understand what they are going through. This is the quality of empathy and is one of the most important gifts your zodiac sign has been given. Your popularity is justifiably high and people want to help you in return.

14 TUESDAY
Moon Age Day 17   Moon Sign Libra

Others find you to be generous and loving – which means that Pisces is displaying itself to the world in the best possible light. More than a degree of good luck is likely to be attending your actions and it looks as though someone who is in a good position to lift your life in some way is noticing you.

15 WEDNESDAY
Moon Age Day 18   Moon Sign Libra

Both work and your social life have the potential to bring you success at the moment. You may feel that there are a few problems, but in reality some of them don't really exist at all. If you experience any difficulty getting to the end of a task that seems to have lasted for ages, get it done little by little in amongst enjoyable jobs.

16 THURSDAY
Moon Age Day 19   Moon Sign Scorpio

The sort of fun you are seeking today might be unavailable but that doesn't mean you shouldn't look for it. In fact, you may be able to pep things up yourself and could have what it takes to make an impression. Pisces is a very understated sign, which is why people take notice when you do turn up the volume.

17 FRIDAY
Moon Age Day 20   Moon Sign Scorpio

Matters undertaken in partnerships look likely to improve and it doesn't matter if these are of a professional or a personal nature. Almost anyone can be of use to you at the moment and it is clear that your mixture of intuition and common sense is what is leading you forward. Expect to receive some messages from people you don't see very often.

18 SATURDAY
Moon Age Day 21   Moon Sign Scorpio

A helping hand can be quite important to you at this time and offers you the chance to get ahead in something you didn't really think you were good at. Seek out those who are in the know and if you are deciding on some new sort of hobby, it's vital to make sure everything is in place before you get started.

19 SUNDAY
Moon Age Day 22   Moon Sign Sagittarius

Whenever you are involved in any group work around this time you find you can shine like a bright star. It isn't that you leap to the front with aggressive determination to be the best of the bunch but rather that your great co-operation and team spirit stands you in good stead. At work you could find rules and regulations to be a drag.

20 MONDAY
Moon Age Day 23   Moon Sign Sagittarius

This would be a good time to surround yourself with friends. The planetary aspects that lead to personal and professional success are not so numerous right now and so a degree of rest would be sensible, if you can manage it. If you want to bask in the glory of things you have been doing up to now, then why not? Your popularity isn't in doubt.

21 TUESDAY
Moon Age Day 24   Moon Sign Capricorn

Your ego is definitely in the ascendant and should remain so for a few days yet. There is just a slight chance that you might be pushing yourself forward too much. One of the things that people really like about you is your humility. Turn it up to full pitch today and you will reap the rewards in due course.

22 WEDNESDAY
Moon Age Day 25   Moon Sign Capricorn

You may tend to let others overshadow you today but it is plain that you know what you are doing. The fact is that you sometimes deliberately take a back seat because that's the way you get others on your side. Pisces needs to be loved and always being at the top of the tree is a place you find too lonely.

23 THURSDAY
Moon Age Day 26   Moon Sign Capricorn

Something very exciting may be about to come along! Perhaps it's a project you started some time ago or it might just be that you are anxious to get ahead generally. Whatever you undertake, you can now do it with aplomb. There are gains to be made at work and maybe a new job in the pipeline if you are between positions.

24 FRIDAY
Moon Age Day 27   Moon Sign Aquarius

Trends suggest that money-wise you should find things coming together even better than you expected. Of course this depends whether or not you even choose to look at such matters today. Certainly there is plenty else that could occupy your mind and you won't be stuck for exciting ways to have a good time.

25 SATURDAY
Moon Age Day 28   Moon Sign Aquarius

This could turn out to be an emotionally tense time and a period during which you will have to look at things in a logical way. This isn't always easy for Pisces but it is possible that you are likely to jump to unnecessary confusions otherwise. If you are in doubt about anything, ask someone you consider to be wise.

26 SUNDAY
Moon Age Day 29   Moon Sign Pisces

Press ahead with major plans and allow others to do what comes naturally to them. You are inclined to work alongside those you care for, whether friends or relatives, but you can't live their lives for them. In any case, there are times when Pisces needs to think and act in isolation. This is such a period.

27 MONDAY
Moon Age Day 0   Moon Sign Pisces

You should be preparing to put new initiatives into action and there isn't much doubt about your ability to get ahead in a very positive way. The lunar high is the icing on the cake today and adds to a wealth of good planetary positions that are around you at present. Your creative potential is especially good right now.

28 TUESDAY
Moon Age Day 1   Moon Sign Aries

This may turn out to be the luckiest day of the month but don't push things because you don't need to. Ease into the day as if you were driving a very powerful car around a fast track. You have all the skill you need to get to the finish post without even breaking into a sweat. You are particularly good in professional matters today.

29 WEDNESDAY
Moon Age Day 2   Moon Sign Aries

There are certain pitfalls to be faced today where finances are concerned. This could be enough to ensure that you don't sign contracts or take on credit agreements unless you are absolutely sure you are doing the right thing. It might be sensible to ask the advice of someone who is either older or more worldly-wise.

30 THURSDAY
Moon Age Day 3   Moon Sign Taurus

Today you can expect personality clashes to crop up in group situations and you do need to be sure that you are not treading on the toes of someone you really rate. Think before you act or speak and be willing to learn from the experience of others. Your confidence grows gradually throughout the day and into the evening.

31 FRIDAY
Moon Age Day 4   Moon Sign Taurus

The recent rather productive period could slacken somewhat and although things should be going fairly well, you might feel as if you are crawling along. Be patient because it isn't given to your sign to keep up a hectic pace indefinitely. You need frequent periods in which you can recharge your batteries – like today for example.

April

2017

Your Month at a Glance

⊕ = Opportunities are around   ⊖ = Be on the defensive   ● = Life is pretty ordinary

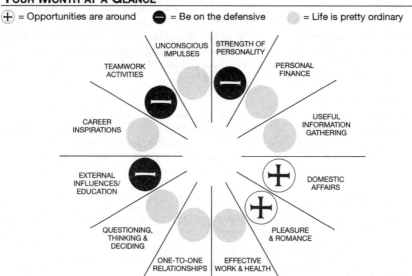

UNCONSCIOUS IMPULSES

STRENGTH OF PERSONALITY

TEAMWORK ACTIVITIES

PERSONAL FINANCE

CAREER INSPIRATIONS

USEFUL INFORMATION GATHERING

EXTERNAL INFLUENCES/ EDUCATION

DOMESTIC AFFAIRS

QUESTIONING, THINKING & DECIDING

PLEASURE & ROMANCE

ONE-TO-ONE RELATIONSHIPS

EFFECTIVE WORK & HEALTH

April Highs and Lows

Here I show you how the rhythms of the Moon will affect you this month. Like the tide, your energies and abilities will rise and fall with its pattern. When it is above the centre line, go for it, when it is below, you should be resting.

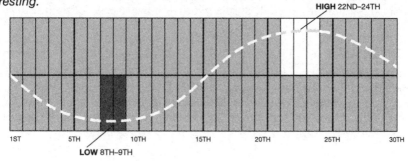

HIGH 22ND–24TH

1ST   5TH   10TH   15TH   20TH   25TH   30TH

LOW 8TH–9TH

1 SATURDAY
Moon Age Day 5   Moon Sign Gemini

Attracting the good things in life won't be difficult this weekend and for once you recognise the value of a little luxury in your life. If someone wants to make a fuss of you, it might be churlish to refuse their kindness. In an artistic sense you show good judgement today so it might be a good time to think about something decorative – perhaps buy a new picture for your home?

2 SUNDAY
Moon Age Day 6   Moon Sign Gemini

The Sun is now in your solar second house, which assists most moneymaking and financial enterprises. Put your thinking cap on for the week ahead because there will be some extra cash available if you simply approach matters in the right way. Other trends suggest that people you haven't seen for a while might be turning up over the next few days.

3 MONDAY
Moon Age Day 7   Moon Sign Cancer

With the domestic area of your life apparently very fulfilling at the moment, and also the chance to make significant progress at work you can get the best of both worlds now. Trends also suggest that a journey taken now, especially a long one, might give you the means to broaden your horizons.

4 TUESDAY
Moon Age Day 8   Moon Sign Cancer

Despite the fact that you keenly feel a number of obligations bearing down on you, today is good for all intellectual pursuits. Your mind is crystal clear and enables you to think through or around any number of potential obstacles. On the way, you are stretching yourself, which has to be a good thing under present trends.

5 WEDNESDAY
Moon Age Day 9   Moon Sign Leo

Social matters are positively highlighted today, and it seems that you will be in a co-operative mood. Much of the joy you experience today comes from what you can do on behalf of others. This is fairly typical of the sign of Pisces and brings a fulfilling period, during which you feel a sense of rightness and balance.

6 THURSDAY
Moon Age Day 10   Moon Sign Leo

Your practical skills are well emphasised at this time. It is possible there are jobs around the house that you will want to undertake yourself, even if you have never tackled them before. With increasing belief in your ability and some positive support from your partner or family members, now is the time to get stuck in.

7 FRIDAY
Moon Age Day 11   Moon Sign Leo

What matters for today is your versatility. People are turning to you for help and advice of a sort they feel only you can offer. The end of this working week may be good from a financial point of view, particularly as a result of actions you took some time ago which are only now bearing fruit.

8 SATURDAY
Moon Age Day 12   Moon Sign Virgo

There may be strong emotions to deal with today, though few of them are likely to be exhibited by you. It seems as though everyone has a unique and somewhat awkward point of view, which itself could lead to some disagreements. As usual, you will be expected to play the mediator.

9 SUNDAY
Moon Age Day 13   Moon Sign Virgo

You can be quite demanding in the personality stakes today, which isn't at all the normal state of affairs for Pisces. In addition, it looks as though you will be willing to push your way to the front of any queue and might even come across as being a little bossy. None of this is a problem but it could surprise a few people.

10 MONDAY   ☿
Moon Age Day 14   Moon Sign Libra

It is time to get down to business and to look very carefully at the practical side of life. You clearly have your thinking head on at the moment and will be easily able to deal with problems that are stumping others. Romance shows itself around this time, though it remains to be seen whether you have the time to notice it.

11 TUESDAY   ☿
Moon Age Day 15   Moon Sign Libra

Personal and intimate subject matter brings out the best in you today. It is likely that you will be able to enjoy the support of loved ones, together with special friends in whom you put a high degree of trust. Committing yourself to new projects might not be all that easy today but should prove simpler tomorrow.

12 WEDNESDAY   ☿
Moon Age Day 16   Moon Sign Scorpio

This is a period during which intimate and private matters should be a source of emotional fulfilment, always an important factor in the life of a Piscean. There could be reasons to celebrate as a result of events within the family and in this mood you will be the first one to put out the flags.

13 THURSDAY ☿ *Moon Age Day 17 Moon Sign Scorpio*

You can easily achieve any reasonable objectives you set yourself today, though you could also be inclined to retreat into yourself if you feel threatened in any way. By far the best response to any slight difficulties would be to face them squarely but this course of action won't be too easy for the moment.

14 FRIDAY ☿ *Moon Age Day 18 Moon Sign Scorpio*

Your chart today reveals a pronounced tendency to be critical today. Fortunately, you exercise this quality only when you are faced with important decisions. Your ability to appraise situations means that you will not walk blindly into anything that could lead to trouble. This is especially important in terms of financial commitments.

15 SATURDAY ☿ *Moon Age Day 19 Moon Sign Sagittarius*

Today can be especially progressive on the financial front, even if you are not actually taking any specific action. A greater understanding of how you should proceed in the future gives you cause to realise you will be better off than you thought. You certainly have not been too optimistic, a fact that becomes obvious now.

16 SUNDAY ☿ *Moon Age Day 20 Moon Sign Sagittarius*

Life should be on a stable footing today and some gains may come in as a result of past efforts and plans that are just starting to mature now. A consideration for the feelings of others is never far from the front of your mind and that certainly seems to be the case at the moment. Positive influences come from the direction of friends.

17 MONDAY ☿ *Moon Age Day 21 Moon Sign Capricorn*

This should be a slightly more settled time in financial terms and there is new scope for improvement to little details in your life. Some Pisceans will be thinking about major alterations in terms of home surroundings, with a few even considering the possibility of a change of abode in the very near future.

18 TUESDAY ☿ *Moon Age Day 22 Moon Sign Capricorn*

Though you are likely to spend rather more than you probably should at this stage of the month, you might also find that some cash is coming in from relatively unexpected directions, which compensates somewhat for what is going out. You can't rely on this trend absolutely, so still take care to avoid too much outlay.

19 WEDNESDAY ☿   *Moon Age Day 23   Moon Sign Capricorn*

Your powers of attraction with regard to the finer things of life are good, though there is also a very spiritual element to your nature right now that doesn't care very much for worldly possessions. These are conflicting qualities that you have to resolve as best you can. Meanwhile, friends will be urging you to have a splurge of some sort.

20 THURSDAY ☿   *Moon Age Day 24   Moon Sign Aquarius*

The Sun enters your solar third house today so you can expect a month ahead that brings plenty of comings and goings. You will be chattier than usual and extremely friendly to anyone you meet. As far as today is concerned, you are likely to spend some time helping a person for whom you have a soft spot.

21 FRIDAY ☿   *Moon Age Day 25   Moon Sign Aquarius*

Whilst spirits and inspiration might be somewhat lacking for the moment, you are clearly looking ahead and planning carefully. It is only really the position of your twelfth house Moon that makes you rather reluctant to act. By tomorrow everything comes good for you but today some patience is required.

22 SATURDAY ☿   *Moon Age Day 26   Moon Sign Pisces*

You have all the support you require today with which to push your ideas forward. The tendency to retreat into your own little world now disappears and you find yourself happy to be in the social flow and taking your place in the world. The lunar high should also bestow a greater degree of luck.

23 SUNDAY ☿   *Moon Age Day 27   Moon Sign Pisces*

Competition is easily outwitted as you take on incentives and are able to see all too clearly the nature of the path that lies before you. On a personal level, the number of compliments coming in at the moment bolsters your confidence and makes you able to react in a positive and even assertive way.

24 MONDAY ☿   *Moon Age Day 28   Moon Sign Pisces*

This is a time during which you need to look ahead with faith that things are going to work out the way you wish. Don't be fooled by people telling you what they think is right for you. In all probability you will make it plain to almost everyone that your ideas are the best ones and you certainly want to have some fun today.

25 TUESDAY ☿ *Moon Age Day 0 Moon Sign Aries*

You should be on top form in all practical matters but now suddenly less inclined to get involved in deep heart-to-hearts. This change of tack isn't all that surprising bearing in mind planetary trends as they stand. If there are any work-based decisions that presently need to be made, today could be the best time.

26 WEDNESDAY ☿ *Moon Age Day 1 Moon Sign Aries*

Close ties and personal relationships are once again on your mind and prove to be the most important aspects of the day. It is true that as the day advances your thoughts will be turning more and more towards practical issues and by the evening you could discover reserves of energy you hadn't recognised earlier in the day.

27 THURSDAY ☿ *Moon Age Day 2 Moon Sign Taurus*

Idealism is a powerful component of your nature at the best of times but this is especially well indicated now. You can expect trends to help you to get far more done today than you might have expected and shouldn't be in the least fazed by having to do several different things at the same time. You might have to wait for friends to catch up with you, though!

28 FRIDAY ☿ *Moon Age Day 3 Moon Sign Taurus*

There seems to be no better way of getting ahead than by sticking to what you know for the moment. Although you might want to push the bounds of the possible, the best progress comes from sticking to what you know you can achieve and not through forcing yourself to try things that go against the grain.

29 SATURDAY ☿ *Moon Age Day 4 Moon Sign Gemini*

You should be in a much better position to call the shots now, particularly if you happen to be a weekend worker. If you are in a position to relax, it is highly likely that you will find some very dynamic way of doing so. Sporting Pisceans are in the very best position of all and can easily get to the finishing line first.

30 SUNDAY ☿ *Moon Age Day 5 Moon Sign Gemini*

You can look forward to newcomers in your life, especially on a social level. Although you may want to let the whole world know how much you love a certain person, this might not be the best time to be wearing your heart on your sleeve. Temper your emotions or at least hide them from people you don't think you can trust.

May 2017

Your Month at a Glance

⊕ = Opportunities are around   ⊖ = Be on the defensive   ◯ = Life is pretty ordinary

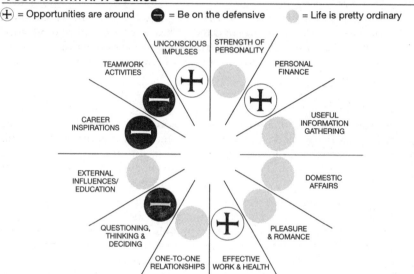

- UNCONSCIOUS IMPULSES
- STRENGTH OF PERSONALITY
- TEAMWORK ACTIVITIES
- PERSONAL FINANCE
- CAREER INSPIRATIONS
- USEFUL INFORMATION GATHERING
- EXTERNAL INFLUENCES/ EDUCATION
- DOMESTIC AFFAIRS
- QUESTIONING, THINKING & DECIDING
- PLEASURE & ROMANCE
- ONE-TO-ONE RELATIONSHIPS
- EFFECTIVE WORK & HEALTH

May Highs and Lows

Here I show you how the rhythms of the Moon will affect you this month. Like the tide, your energies and abilities will rise and fall with its pattern. When it is above the centre line, go for it, when it is below, you should be resting.

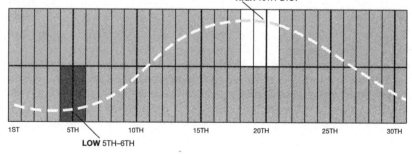

HIGH 19TH–21ST

1ST   5TH   10TH   15TH   20TH   25TH   30TH

LOW 5TH–6TH

1 MONDAY ☿ *Moon Age Day 6   Moon Sign Cancer*

In an optimistic frame of mind today, your confidence in your own abilities mean that there isn't much at which you will fail. People notice the new you and are anxious to back a winner. This increases your popularity and might mean a good deal of attention coming your way during the week.

2 TUESDAY ☿ *Moon Age Day 7   Moon Sign Cancer*

The potential for attracting money is sluggish now and isn't anywhere near as good as it was only a few days ago. Still, you can tell yourself that the most important things in life have no monetary value. This is the Piscean spiritual ideal – but it might not prevent you from wanting those new shoes.

3 WEDNESDAY ☿ *Moon Age Day 8   Moon Sign Leo*

Pisces is now in a very co-operative frame of mind. If you are not working today, you could definitely benefit from some time spent with groups of people who share your ideas and objectives. Later in the day you will find yourself in a very sociable frame of mind and won't want to spend this Wednesday evening indoors.

4 THURSDAY *Moon Age Day 9   Moon Sign Leo*

Although you might have to seek advice today, trends suggest that the general pace is not slackened at all. This is an especially good day for making money and for bringing reluctant people round to your own, unique, point of view. Along the way, you should prove to be both entertaining and disarming.

5 FRIDAY *Moon Age Day 10   Moon Sign Virgo*

It would be a good idea to play safe in professional matters and to defer to the wisdom of people who know more about certain facts than you do. Don't allow your perception of your own limitations to affect your confidence in yourself. You know what you can achieve when you put your mind to it, so stick to that.

6 SATURDAY *Moon Age Day 11   Moon Sign Virgo*

Getting your own way in money matters could turn out to be rather easier than you had expected. Simply turn on the charm, put forward a good, reasoned case and wait for the result. A degree of frugality may be necessary in the short-term, if only to prove to others you can practically live on fresh air. The lunar low makes this easy.

7 SUNDAY
Moon Age Day 12   Moon Sign Libra

Today is all about communication and what you can gain from this two-way process. Your level of decisiveness and confidence may not be exactly what you would wish but this won't matter if you realise how much support you genuinely have. You may decide the time is right to make specific changes to working patterns.

8 MONDAY
Moon Age Day 13   Moon Sign Libra

Others will find you to be very talkative today and will find it difficult to keep up with your active mind and quick tongue. You do seem to be experiencing many extremes at this time but you cope with them well. Certain family members could prove to be a little argumentative but this will not worry you unduly.

9 TUESDAY
Moon Age Day 14   Moon Sign Libra

Now the demands of the big wide world show themselves more and you will respond to the present planetary trends, which make you chatty, anxious to please and keen to get on in life. Although there are elements of domestic bliss still tugging at you, the more excitement-loving Pisces is likely to win through.

10 WEDNESDAY
Moon Age Day 15   Moon Sign Scorpio

There are only so many things you can control at once, so if you are tiring under the strain of it all, delegate some of the responsibility and try to take a break. It looks as though there will be people around who are only too willing to lend a hand. Meanwhile, look for new and interesting ways to fill your leisure hours.

11 THURSDAY
Moon Age Day 16   Moon Sign Scorpio

You should be looking and feeling at your best today. Socially and romantically, there are many situations that seem tailor-made to suit your needs. Try to keep confrontations of any sort to a minimum and focus on love and romance, which is number-one on the agenda of many sons and daughters of Pisces now.

12 FRIDAY
Moon Age Day 17   Moon Sign Sagittarius

This is a time when you will be actively seeking to broaden your horizons in just about any way you can manage. Those Pisceans who have chosen to take a holiday around now are probably the luckiest, but there are gains to be made even if you can't get away from the usual routines. Pace yourself so you have energy in reserve for a fun Friday night.

13 SATURDAY
Moon Age Day 18   Moon Sign Sagittarius

You can expect to get the very best from family members and people you care for even if it isn't possible for you to be at home quite as much as you might wish. A lot of the pressure you feel at the moment could be related to being in the limelight, a place where you invariably feel ill at ease. Try to step away from the attention if you can.

14 SUNDAY
Moon Age Day 19   Moon Sign Sagittarius

What a good day this would be for entertaining at home. It is clear that you are now at your vibrant best when in your own environment and will welcome others with open arms. Maybe you will dream up an impromptu party or a gathering of some other sort. Avoid thinking too much about events beyond your own front door now.

15 MONDAY
Moon Age Day 20   Moon Sign Capricorn

Quick thinking comes in handy today and you won't have any difficulty functioning at full strength. Your mind works quickly, though it is also sometimes drawn to places you care for deeply and which you might not have seen for a while. You should be feeling generally comfortable with personal and romantic attachments.

16 TUESDAY
Moon Age Day 21   Moon Sign Capricorn

Today you show yourself to be outgoing and enthusiastic, though you could suffer a little from inadequate planning and will need to step in and take action if someone you consider a rival seems to be getting ahead of you. Pisceans who are presently in full time education can expect to be doing well with studies now.

17 WEDNESDAY
Moon Age Day 22   Moon Sign Aquarius

The focus is now upon communications in the outside world. This is a favourable period for important negotiations and discussions, and a time during which you can get what you want, though only with determination and belief. You may turn your attention to comfort and security later in the day.

18 THURSDAY
Moon Age Day 23   Moon Sign Aquarius

Domestic matters could tie you down somewhat right now and you would be best not getting too involved in situations you presently can't or won't alter. Younger people especially could turn out to be quite frustrating in their objectives and desires, some of which directly contradict your own. A little Piscean patience might be called for.

19 FRIDAY
Moon Age Day 24   Moon Sign Pisces

Personal objectives are definitely worth pursuing at this time and you should not let go of an ambition or dream until you have what you want. The lunar high gives you energy and a much greater determination than usual, whilst the assistance that comes from the direction of others might be surprising on occasion.

20 SATURDAY
Moon Age Day 25   Moon Sign Pisces

Your spirits are very much alive now and there are many practical gains to be made by simply keeping your eye on the ball. A happy time is likely and you won't go short of the sort of attention that gives you more confidence in yourself. The level of physical energy you register today is extremely high.

21 SUNDAY
Moon Age Day 26   Moon Sign Pisces

You can afford to be slightly more ambitious in your personal aims and should be going for gold at every possible opportunity. Not everyone is presently on your side it's true, but you do have a really good ability to persuade others to follow your lead. It is definitely worth talking, talking and talking again in order to get what you want.

22 MONDAY
Moon Age Day 27   Moon Sign Aries

You won't have a great deal of patience with financial restrictions and will desire a higher degree of freedom at present. Woe-betide anyone who tries to force you into any sort of mould because it just won't work. Have some patience with family members who are going slightly astray and listen to them.

23 TUESDAY
Moon Age Day 28   Moon Sign Aries

Communication matters put you in the picture today so it is very important to keep talking to anyone who will listen and respond. You may be researching something or perhaps involved in higher education. If so, make certain that you concentrate your efforts at the moment because a significant breakthrough is possible.

24 WEDNESDAY
Moon Age Day 29   Moon Sign Taurus

This would be an excellent time in which to put your persuasive tongue to work. There are people around who are very influenced by what you have to say and at work you should be able to move matters forward quite progressively. Even casual conversations can have far-reaching implications.

25 THURSDAY
Moon Age Day 0   Moon Sign Taurus

Personal and domestic concerns now bring out the best in you, though there are social bonuses around too, probably later in the day. Concern for family members, which could have been running quite high of late, is not so marked at present, leaving you extra time to spend in doing what suits you personally.

26 FRIDAY
Moon Age Day 1   Moon Sign Gemini

The emphasis for now is on busy communication, though others might find you just a little too talkative at the moment. It's important not to labour points too much and if you remember the general rule for now, which is to spread yourself around as much as you can, you won't go far wrong. A friend may need some very specific advice.

27 SATURDAY
Moon Age Day 2   Moon Sign Gemini

Certain compromises can be rather more difficult to make than you would wish. In the end you could decide that you are better off sticking to your guns, especially in professional matters. People don't give you the time to think things through clearly, which means there isn't quite as much room to manoeuvre as you need.

28 SUNDAY
Moon Age Day 3   Moon Sign Cancer

Feelings and emotions tend to be an open book to you at the moment and you have nothing to hide. Your attitude can be quite disarming as far as those around you are concerned and you will probably discover that they are as truthful as you. A new understanding is possible with someone you haven't always understood well.

29 MONDAY
Moon Age Day 4   Moon Sign Cancer

There's a greater tendency towards hustle and bustle as this week gets started. The potential for excitement is present but it really depends on the way you respond to the stimulus coming in from outside. Casual conversations can lead to quite significant forward progress in terms of money.

30 TUESDAY
Moon Age Day 5   Moon Sign Leo

This is likely to be a day of busy demands and responsibilities. Fortunately you are in the right state of mind to take these in your stride and can work through a mountain of tasks slowly and steadily. You almost certainly will find that you need to take a little time to yourself at some stage during the day.

31 WEDNESDAY
Moon Age Day 6   Moon Sign Leo

With a slight lull in the pace of activities, your mind could turn towards house and home. What a good time this would be for entertaining and maybe for throwing a dinner party. Much of the enjoyment you experience today is likely to be associated with domestic rather than professional matters.

June
2017

YOUR MONTH AT A GLANCE

(+) = Opportunities are around   ● = Be on the defensive   ○ = Life is pretty ordinary

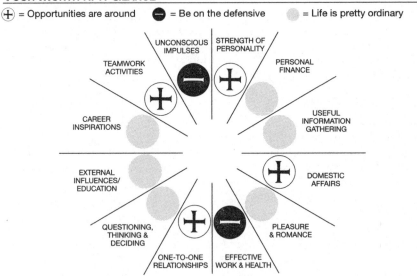

- UNCONSCIOUS IMPULSES
- STRENGTH OF PERSONALITY
- TEAMWORK ACTIVITIES
- PERSONAL FINANCE
- CAREER INSPIRATIONS
- USEFUL INFORMATION GATHERING
- EXTERNAL INFLUENCES/ EDUCATION
- DOMESTIC AFFAIRS
- QUESTIONING, THINKING & DECIDING
- PLEASURE & ROMANCE
- ONE-TO-ONE RELATIONSHIPS
- EFFECTIVE WORK & HEALTH

JUNE HIGHS AND LOWS

Here I show you how the rhythms of the Moon will affect you this month. Like the tide, your energies and abilities will rise and fall with its pattern. When it is above the centre line, go for it, when it is below, you should be resting.

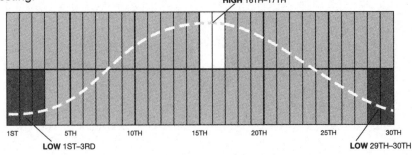

HIGH 16TH–17TH

LOW 1ST–3RD

LOW 29TH–30TH

1ST   5TH   10TH   15TH   20TH   25TH   30TH

I THURSDAY
Moon Age Day 7   Moon Sign Virgo

Your daily life could become somewhat disorganised to say the least. The culprit is the lunar low though it also brings a good deal of amusement this time round as you discover just how funny you can be when things start to go haywire. There is little or no animosity in your life right now, which is comfortable and gratifying.

2 FRIDAY
Moon Age Day 8   Moon Sign Virgo

This is another day on which you won't feel like competing as much as you have done during the last few weeks. Have a rest and take the opportunity to look around yourself. Your confidence might be low now, but you are already planning some sort of coup for later and as long as you don't try to push ahead too soon, all should be well.

3 SATURDAY
Moon Age Day 9   Moon Sign Virgo

Pisces turns very nostalgic now and could spend as much time looking back as it does at the present or the future. If there are valuable lessons to be gained that's fine but what you don't want is to get stuck into a cycle of activity simply to replicate matters that you should consider finished and done.

4 SUNDAY
Moon Age Day 10   Moon Sign Libra

Communications come to the fore today and you get by extremely well if you keep speaking. You may not always know exactly what you are talking about but in a way that doesn't matter. You are in the middle of a phase during which you could charm the birds down from the trees but not if you fail to open up and talk frankly.

5 MONDAY
Moon Age Day 11   Moon Sign Libra

A missive – perhaps a letter or email – from far away might lift your spirits at the beginning of this week. You will also be chattier than may have been the case for a number of days. There are potential gains to be made from simply being in the right place at the right time but your deep insights are also part of the scenario.

6 THURSDAY
Moon Age Day 12   Moon Sign Scorpio

Stand by for a few potential irritations today, particularly where work is concerned. Maybe this comes as a result of frustration because you can't get others to see your point of view. Remember that there is always more than one way of looking at any situation and show some of that stoical Piscean patience.

7 WEDNESDAY
Moon Age Day 13   Moon Sign Scorpio

The focus now is definitely on your love life and romance generally. This is likely to be a very positive period with much of what you have been looking for likely to come your way. Don't spoil this by spending more time than you have to out there in the more practical and go-getting world.

8 THURSDAY
Moon Age Day 14   Moon Sign Sagittarius

In terms of your general ego, today should turn out to be very interesting. This is one of the best days of the month for proving how much your own personality can influence that of other people. Discussions at home should go well and probably offer much more in a personal sense than outside influences.

9 FRIDAY
Moon Age Day 15   Moon Sign Sagittarius

Personal relationships could be somewhat less harmonious than you would wish, although this doesn't seem to have a great deal to do with you. It's important to speak the truth at the moment, even if that means upsetting someone else. All the same, you can find ways to be tactful if you put your mind to it.

10 SATURDAY
Moon Age Day 16   Moon Sign Sagittarius

The accent today should be firmly on pleasure, with plenty of people lending a hand to help you have a good time. There might not be many hours to think about the practicalities of life but you won't worry about that. Pisces is now more than happy to be the life and soul of any party that is taking place.

11 SUNDAY
Moon Age Day 17   Moon Sign Capricorn

Much of your energy today is piled into situations you see as being personally important. It is just possible that this means less attention being put in the direction of family members. It would be good to offer a little reassurance to them because those you love are very used to seeing your warm and attentive side.

12 MONDAY
Moon Age Day 18   Moon Sign Capricorn

Since professional matters appear to be progressive enough, the chances are that you will want to put some pep into your out-of-work activities. Concern for the underdog is big in your thinking right now and you show your usual Piscean concern for charities that support people who are having a hard time in their lives.

13 TUESDAY
Moon Age Day 19   Moon Sign Aquarius

You can put the finishing touches to one or two jobs today but it will almost certainly occur to you that you are not working at your very best. However, the deeper recesses of your mind are definitely engaged and your intuition appears to be second to none. It should certainly be easy to see through to the true motives of others.

14 WEDNESDAY
Moon Age Day 20   Moon Sign Aquarius

Trends suggest that you will now be much more boisterous than you usually are, and certainly than you have been of late. You stand out in a crowd and can give a very good account of yourself. It is obvious that you are also quite adventurous and daring at present, not a word that is often seen by the side of Pisces.

15 THURSDAY
Moon Age Day 21   Moon Sign Aquarius

Look out for some overall improvements at work, or perhaps a better ability to concentrate if you are engaged in education. The better times are really down to you and the way your mind is presently working. Don't be too quick to listen to gossip today because a lot of it isn't really worth the effort.

16 FRIDAY
Moon Age Day 22   Moon Sign Pisces

You need to follow your instincts today because with a host of supporting planetary positions, together with the lunar high, you shouldn't go wrong. This can be a really interesting sort of day and one packed with variety. Fresh starts are a must, together with new ways of looking at old situations.

17 SATURDAY
Moon Age Day 23   Moon Sign Pisces

Don't be afraid to aim high or to take some chances at the beginning of this weekend. You find yourself on a very important springboard and with a very positive sort of period in front of you, it's time to jump. The attitude of colleagues especially is likely to be surprising and more than useful. Friends are demanding but sweet.

18 SUNDAY
Moon Age Day 24   Moon Sign Aries

Relations with family members are now strengthened by a number of astrological factors and if there is something you need to ask for in the way of a favour, this could be the best time of all in which to do it. Relying on friends may be less advisable for today at least because you could find that they are too busy to lend assistance.

19 MONDAY
Moon Age Day 25   Moon Sign Aries

You could now be pulled between your desire to be with loved ones and your need to make contact with the world at large. There isn't much that makes you feel really wonderful just now but this is a state of affairs that won't last long. Personalities of one sort or another might be entering your life sometime soon.

20 TUESDAY
Moon Age Day 26   Moon Sign Taurus

A period of intense feelings and emotional conflicts now comes along, though has less of a part to play in your life if you are aware of its presence. Don't rise to the bait of someone who is spoiling for a row and then you will be the winner from the word go. At work you may need to do the same job more than once.

21 WEDNESDAY
Moon Age Day 27   Moon Sign Taurus

You need to find time today to go off and explore the world as much as you can. There is plenty to see and any number of interesting people around. This is not a Wednesday during which practical or professional matters should be allowed to get in the way of simply doing what seems like special fun.

22 THURSDAY
Moon Age Day 28   Moon Sign Gemini

Trends change and you need to get on top of work matters as soon as you can this morning. If this isn't possible, you might have to rely on the help of someone else to get your house in order. Routines could seem quite comfortable at a time when you probably won't want to be pushing your horizons too much.

23 FRIDAY
Moon Age Day 29   Moon Sign Gemini

Your confidence is increasing and the Sun, now in your solar fifth house, is part of the reason for this. You tend to get your own way quite easily in romantic matters and from a general leisure and pleasure point of view could well be starting the weekend a day early. Socially speaking, you are good to know.

24 SATURDAY
Moon Age Day 0   Moon Sign Cancer

You should prove to be more than modestly successful in almost anything you choose to take on at the moment. Getting ahead professionally still isn't all that likely, as much as anything because this is a Saturday. What not ring the changes altogether and get away from everything? What a good time this would be to take a break.

25 SUNDAY
Moon Age Day 1   Moon Sign Cancer

Others might be able to deceive you, but only today. Show a little caution and don't be quite as trusting as might sometimes be the case. People you don't see everyday are now likely to be cropping up in your life all the time and you might also be invited to take part in something that has been a mystery to you in the past.

26 MONDAY
Moon Age Day 2   Moon Sign Leo

Be careful not to overlook financial obligations today. You need to put documents into the necessary envelopes and get them off, if only because you are likely to be both busy and slightly forgetful at the moment. Socially speaking, things probably could not be better, with plenty of opportunities to get out and meet people.

27 TUESDAY
Moon Age Day 3   Moon Sign Leo

Getting your own way at the moment is generally a matter of turning on the charm, which is never difficult for Pisces. You are displaying the very best of what you can be and so should enjoy a really good day. Events may prove to be spiritually enlightening, though pleasures are probably very simple.

28 WEDNESDAY
Moon Age Day 4   Moon Sign Leo

You could be the main attraction wherever you go today. Make the most of it because for the next couple of days quieter times are in store. There are possible gains to be made financially, though this isn't the best time for gambling unless you can be very certain of the outcome which, let's face it, isn't usually the case with gambling! The best advice is to play it safe.

29 THURSDAY
Moon Age Day 5   Moon Sign Virgo

You now have to endure the two days of the lunar low that comes along at this time. In fact this need not be a trial at all. Just remember to stay away from anything sensational and don't take unnecessary risks. In any case, you might find quiet pursuits more interesting whilst present trends are in place.

30 FRIDAY
Moon Age Day 6   Moon Sign Virgo

If you take life one step at a time you might even come to enjoy the fact that you don't have to think about a dozen different things at the same time. There ought to be time to spend with loved ones and good friends and a certain quiet feel to the period that many people born under the sign of Pisces will actively enjoy.

July

2017

YOUR MONTH AT A GLANCE

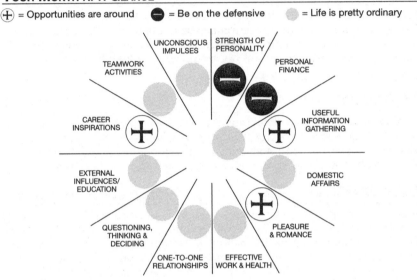

⊕ = Opportunities are around ⊖ = Be on the defensive ⬤ = Life is pretty ordinary

- UNCONSCIOUS IMPULSES
- STRENGTH OF PERSONALITY
- TEAMWORK ACTIVITIES
- PERSONAL FINANCE
- CAREER INSPIRATIONS
- USEFUL INFORMATION GATHERING
- EXTERNAL INFLUENCES/ EDUCATION
- DOMESTIC AFFAIRS
- QUESTIONING, THINKING & DECIDING
- PLEASURE & ROMANCE
- ONE-TO-ONE RELATIONSHIPS
- EFFECTIVE WORK & HEALTH

JULY HIGHS AND LOWS

Here I show you how the rhythms of the Moon will affect you this month. Like the tide, your energies and abilities will rise and fall with its pattern. When it is above the centre line, go for it, when it is below, you should be resting.

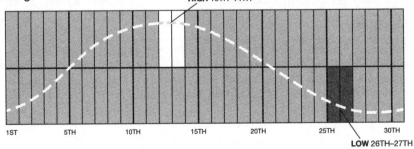

HIGH 13TH–14TH

1ST 5TH 10TH 15TH 20TH 25TH 30TH

LOW 26TH–27TH

1 SATURDAY
Moon Age Day 7   Moon Sign Libra

In a light and optimistic frame of mind now, you are anxious to get to know new people but also very attentive to family members and friends. With such a sociable period in operation it might be rather difficult to actually get anything done in a concrete sense. Never mind, you can easily split your time.

2 SUNDAY
Moon Age Day 8   Moon Sign Libra

Trends suggest that you will feel the need to get ahead with plans today, though you are inclined to realise that this might sometimes require a very considered and careful approach. Today Pisces is likely to be looking around, waiting for the best opportunity to act and then doing all that is necessary to win through.

3 MONDAY
Moon Age Day 9   Moon Sign Scorpio

Certain personal or practical arrangements could quite easily be subject to delay now. You need to remain flexible in your attitude and willing to take a different path at very short notice. Casual conversations can bring unexpected news or some really good ideas you will soon be bursting to put into practice.

4 TUESDAY
Moon Age Day 10   Moon Sign Scorpio

Stick around familiar faces today because you are not quite as adventurous as you were a few days ago. Although you are by no means a shrinking violet, you could be rather inclined to hide behind the bigger personalities of friends. But it doesn't matter what you do, there are people who want to know you better.

5 WEDNESDAY
Moon Age Day 11   Moon Sign Scorpio

Impressing others isn't too difficult today and you will manage to pull the right rabbit out of the hat when it is important to do so. People will trust you a great deal and you might worry just a little in case you let them down. This is most unlikely to happen. Just be yourself and do what feels right.

6 THURSDAY
Moon Age Day 12   Moon Sign Sagittarius

The accent is now less on practical organisation and more on initiative and willpower. Once you have made up your mind very little holds you back at present. You may have to use slightly unorthodox ways of getting what you want from the day but the chances are that you will win through in the end.

7 FRIDAY
Moon Age Day 13   Moon Sign Sagittarius

This would be a great day for family gatherings and for talking over old times. Although you are still progressive and productive, you are more likely to show your sociable side. There are possible gains to be made from sharing some of your innermost thoughts with those you know to be trustworthy.

8 SATURDAY
Moon Age Day 14   Moon Sign Capricorn

When it matters the most you can rely on your instincts today, which are most unlikely to let you down. A few financial pressures are possible this weekend but there are many things you can do that are absolutely free, or which cost very little. Being with friends would be good but even better times involve your partner or spouse.

9 SUNDAY
Moon Age Day 15   Moon Sign Capricorn

It isn't so much that you are following good trends today, more that you are able to create them as you go along. This is especially true in a career sense or with regard to an important personal interest if you are not working at present. Most important of all at the moment is the cheerful mood with which you greet everyone today.

10 MONDAY
Moon Age Day 16   Moon Sign Capricorn

Seek out the new and unusual in life and concentrate on using the natural detective qualities within your deep Piscean nature. Anything that captivates your interest at present is grist to the mill, the most important fact being that you see clearly through any form of subterfuge to the real heart of the matter.

11 TUESDAY
Moon Age Day 17   Moon Sign Aquarius

Although you are a strong participant in the game of life, you also have the power to stand back from situations and to look at them dispassionately. This part of the week brings its own brand of fun, even if your sense of humour at present is slightly off the wall and distinctly unusual when seen from the perspective of others.

12 WEDNESDAY
Moon Age Day 18   Moon Sign Aquarius

Having friends close to you now is very important and makes you feel better about yourself. Although there could be one or two slightly sticky situations to get through today, you keep a smile on your face and show how positive you are capable of being. Your confidence might be lacking but nobody would ever guess it.

13 THURSDAY
Moon Age Day 19   Moon Sign Pisces

It is unlikely you will have to work very hard to win anyone's support today. The Moon is in your zodiac sign and there are also several other planetary positions working in your favour. If you can't get through everything you want to do quickly enough to leave time for fun, leave some of it until later.

14 FRIDAY
Moon Age Day 20   Moon Sign Pisces

Along comes renewed vitality, a determination to succeed and far more drive than has sometimes been the case so far this year. This is potentially a day for good luck, even if you are creating some of it. There are gains to be made at work, perhaps as a result of the influence you have on others.

15 SATURDAY
Moon Age Day 21   Moon Sign Aries

Today has its ups and downs, the more so if you have to work on a Saturday. Left to your own devices, you would probably relax a great deal and you might even look for some luxury. If responsibilities simply will not allow you to be selfish in any way, you can at least dream – let's face it, nobody does that better than Pisces.

16 SUNDAY
Moon Age Day 22   Moon Sign Aries

Though the nostalgic side of your personality is stimulated at this time, you will also want to get on with something practical. The two states of mind don't really go hand in hand and this could lead to some slight confusion. By the evening you should have resolved the conundrums and will settle for peace and quiet.

17 MONDAY
Moon Age Day 23   Moon Sign Aries

This is a time during which it is not sensible to force issues too much, especially in the material world. You need to work hard in order to get what you want but you still have to go with the flow. Any tendency to push too hard is likely to lead to an equal and opposite reaction that you would probably wish to avoid.

18 TUESDAY
Moon Age Day 24   Moon Sign Taurus

It seems that industry and general hard work is the order of the day but not because anyone is forcing you down this path. There are astrological trends about that increase your level of energy and which make you ever more determined to win through to objectives that might have seemed impossible only months ago.

19 WEDNESDAY
Moon Age Day 25   Moon Sign Taurus

Focus on relationships today, and especially those that are most important to you. There won't be much difficulty in coming to terms with practical issues but from an emotional point of view you may be rather too sensitive for your own good. If you can, settle for some way of enjoying yourself that is not too physically demanding.

20 THURSDAY
Moon Age Day 26   Moon Sign Gemini

This is a time when you may find yourself getting tied up with material considerations, some of which might go against the grain somewhat. Nevertheless you need to think about money and the way you are going to get more of it in the months ahead. There ought to be time for enjoyment too, so put an hour or so aside to spend with family or friends.

21 FRIDAY
Moon Age Day 27   Moon Sign Gemini

If some material issues seem to put you under pressure at present, it might be best to leave them to one side for now. Concentrate instead on your relationships with family members and on the emotional side of your life. A quieter Pisces is now on display, but maybe only for a few days.

22 SATURDAY
Moon Age Day 28   Moon Sign Cancer

Practical developments are all-important but you may still be happiest to leave some of the details to those around you. If you are at work you might be called upon to make snap decisions and even though this isn't necessarily easy for you, it will work in your favour if you can only get yourself in the right frame of mind.

23 SUNDAY
Moon Age Day 0   Moon Sign Cancer

On the day the Sun enters your solar sixth house, you can expect to experience a boost to your health and feelings of general wellbeing. If you have been off-colour, this position of the Sun is quite likely to help you to recover. Practical projects and plans for the future are also aided by the presence of the Sun here.

24 MONDAY
Moon Age Day 1   Moon Sign Leo

The pressure is on to take the bull by the horns in some practical or professional way and you had better do so now because by Wednesday the lunar low will prevent you from doing so. You are likely to be busier than ever but will have the consolation of knowing that some quieter days lie in store for you.

25 TUESDAY
Moon Age Day 2   Moon Sign Leo

Not everything goes quite the way you might have planned but you can be reasonably sure that anything to do with love and romance is particularly well accented at the moment. A gradual slowdown becomes apparent as the day advances and you need to get yourself into a steadier and more contemplative state of mind.

26 WEDNESDAY
Moon Age Day 3   Moon Sign Virgo

You can't really expect to be at your most communicative today. The lunar low takes away some of your determination and might make it somewhat difficult to achieve the direct contact with others you might wish. More withdrawn, your attitude is one of patience and your technique is to organise behind the scenes.

27 THURSDAY
Moon Age Day 4   Moon Sign Virgo

Don't be surprised if there are some setbacks today, particularly with regard to projects you see as being important to your future. The delays caused are strictly temporary but they have to be recognised. Instead of ploughing on with things you can't do, concentrate on something smaller that you can achieve successfully.

28 FRIDAY
Moon Age Day 5   Moon Sign Libra

The workplace is favoured at the moment and there might not be quite as much time to spend with your partner or loved ones as you would wish. Specific trends can now make you somewhat absent-minded, so it's important to make a note of birthdays or anniversaries that might be in the offing.

29 SATURDAY
Moon Age Day 6   Moon Sign Libra

Stay close to familiar faces and places this weekend. You will be happiest when in the company of people who make you feel comfortable. You will be feeling particularly sensitive to the needs of those around you and will be displaying all the empathy your sign is capable of mustering. Your creative potential is also now particularly good.

30 SUNDAY
Moon Age Day 7   Moon Sign Libra

Your love life receives its bonuses now but you don't need to try too hard to bring others round to your way of thinking. Don't expect anything too outrageous today. In the main you are happy to accept what comes along but you are not going to be a great pace-setter at the end of this month.

31 MONDAY
Moon Age Day 8   Moon Sign Scorpio

You should be able to find very interesting things to do with yourself at this time and won't easily be convinced that any of your ideas are unworkable. The problem could be that one or two of them are and that those who care for you the most realise the truth. Try to listen carefully to advice and to look at your life objectively.

August 2017

YOUR MONTH AT A GLANCE

⊕ = Opportunities are around   ⊖ = Be on the defensive   ⬤ = Life is pretty ordinary

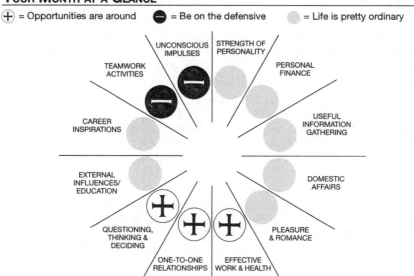

AUGUST HIGHS AND LOWS

Here I show you how the rhythms of the Moon will affect you this month. Like the tide, your energies and abilities will rise and fall with its pattern. When it is above the centre line, go for it, when it is below, you should be resting.

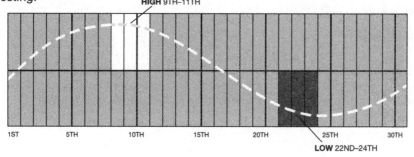

91

1 TUESDAY
Moon Age Day 9   Moon Sign Scorpio

You may have some opportunities for advancement at present, but you will have to look closely to find them. Life isn't especially easy right now but you are competent, discriminating and able to get what you want with perseverance. The more romantic aspects of your life are likely to be quite gratifying.

2 WEDNESDAY
Moon Age Day 10   Moon Sign Sagittarius

This would be an excellent time for co-operative ventures of any sort. Planetary trends in your solar chart makes it easy for you to get on with the people you work or live with, though strangers can appear intimidating on occasions. Keep up your efforts in a specific and important direction.

3 THURSDAY
Moon Age Day 11   Moon Sign Sagittarius

This is still a good period to be making the sort of progress you are definitely looking for at this time. You show good and promising judgement and once you have made up your mind to follow a particular path you won't easily be put off. Inspiration is part of the present package for Pisces today.

4 FRIDAY
Moon Age Day 12   Moon Sign Sagittarius

Don't allow yourself to become involved in needless debates, which won't help your cause and can only serve to confuse already problematic situations. There is help on offer if you want it, though you are likely to be relying on your own efforts and judgement now and so may decide that it is best to continue going it alone.

5 SATURDAY
Moon Age Day 13   Moon Sign Capricorn

The smooth running of practical affairs today is your chief concern, as indeed seems to have been the case for a while now. Although circumstances force you to work within certain confines, you are presently extremely good at solving problems and won't easily be distracted, especially by people you have little respect for.

6 SUNDAY
Moon Age Day 14   Moon Sign Capricorn

Help seems to be available to you today, no matter what you decide to do. There are times when you are responding to necessity, rather than to choice but you can make these enjoyable too. Routines could be a bore, which is why you are doing your best to ring the changes as much as you can.

7 MONDAY
Moon Age Day 15   Moon Sign Aquarius

In personal relationships, it is important not to get too wrapped up in your own ideas, no matter how entrancing they seem to be to you. Use a listening ear and be willing to modify your plans if necessary. A final word of warning for a summer Monday – avoid staying in the same place for too long at a time.

8 TUESDAY
Moon Age Day 16   Moon Sign Aquarius

This is certainly the best potential period for financial gain during August. You tend to act very much on impulse but your sense of humour is fully in place and so if you make a mistake, you can laugh your way out of it. Concern for the underdog is particularly strong at the moment for Pisces so keep an eye open for someone who needs help.

9 WEDNESDAY
Moon Age Day 17   Moon Sign Pisces

As the Moon moves into your zodiac sign, so you find yourself in a positive frame of mind and anxious to get on with things. Your confidence is present in large measure and you shouldn't have any problems bringing people round to your point of view. Best of all, you recognise how important you are to those you hold dear.

10 THURSDAY
Moon Age Day 18   Moon Sign Pisces

Not only the people you know but also individuals you have barely met before conspire to give you a good day. This is not a time for routines and the lunar high demands that you put in that extra bit of effort that can see your successes mount. With good luck on your side, getting along well should be so easy now.

11 FRIDAY
Moon Age Day 19   Moon Sign Pisces

It could be that practical duties are something of a bind today, which is why you tend to shrug them off or delegate someone else to do them if you have the chance. However, there is no way of avoiding certain responsibilities, so you will just have to grit your teeth and get them done as quickly as possible before you can settle into the weekend ahead.

12 SATURDAY
Moon Age Day 20   Moon Sign Aries

Now is as good a time as any take your life into your own hands. You clearly know what you want and have a very good idea about how you are going to get it. Even apparently unfortunate events can turn to your advantage and will give you a racing start as the hot summer days pass.

13 SUNDAY ☿ *Moon Age Day 21   Moon Sign Aries*

Although there may be obstacles to overcome today, you should be able to deal with them easily and leave yourself feeling quite satisfied with your general progress. Your imaginative faculties are especially good right now, which makes it easy for you to look and plan ahead. Friends should prove to be very supportive.

14 MONDAY ☿ *Moon Age Day 22   Moon Sign Taurus*

You may feel pressurised by a domestic chore or a personal decision you have to take. Of course, you could shop around for some timely advice but it would be best to get this from people who are not directly involved. The normal gossip that surrounds you on an average day could prove less than inspiring – unless you are doing the talking.

15 TUESDAY ☿ *Moon Age Day 23   Moon Sign Taurus*

You can't afford to take anything for granted on a practical level today and will need to check all details carefully. If it appears that someone is deliberately throwing obstacles in your path, take the time to stop and consider what is really happening. It's very possible that it is you who is being a little paranoid.

16 WEDNESDAY ☿ *Moon Age Day 24   Moon Sign Gemini*

You need to invest your feelings into the things you are saying now and won't be short of a listening ear. The time has come for a good deal more personal enjoyment than seems to have been possible for a while. If there is a really tedious job to be done, get it out of the way as early in the day as you can.

17 THURSDAY ☿ *Moon Age Day 25   Moon Sign Gemini*

Some Pisceans may notice the beginnings of what could turn out to be a romantic attachment. When you love, you do so totally, so it's important to make certain that your feelings are genuinely reciprocated before you become too involved. At the same time, you need to stay away from gossip of any sort and make up your own mind about people and situations.

18 FRIDAY ☿ *Moon Age Day 26   Moon Sign Cancer*

There could be some tensions in what are normal discussions, partly because you are not looking as fairly at other people's points of view as might usually be the case. Try to stay away from too much decision-making and do what you can to make this a fairly easy-going sort of Friday. Friends expect your help and you will be there for them.

19 SATURDAY ☿   *Moon Age Day 27   Moon Sign Cancer*

This would be an excellent time for communication and is certainly the most potentially productive day for some time. Although you might be slightly nervous about something you have to do, there is no reason why you should show this in your actions. Consideration for others is self-evident all day.

20 SUNDAY ☿   *Moon Age Day 28   Moon Sign Leo*

Communication with others continues to be well highlighted now and it seems as though you have no trouble at all making those around you understand the way you feel. Although you might be nervy on occasions, you will still manage to get what you want from life, with a combination of bravery and barefaced cheek.

21 MONDAY ☿   *Moon Age Day 29   Moon Sign Leo*

Your social talent is going to give you a number of advantages today and you will become an active member of any group to which you already have an attachment. Conforming to expectations as far as certain family members are concerned could prove to be somewhat difficult right now.

22 TUESDAY ☿   *Moon Age Day 0   Moon Sign Virgo*

The road ahead might seem to contain a few pitfalls but it is vital that you don't look at today in isolation. No matter how hard some things might be, you will soon see that this is nothing but a temporary aberration. Travel is well highlighted, leading to a time ahead during which a holiday would go down extremely well.

23 WEDNESDAY ☿   *Moon Age Day 1   Moon Sign Virgo*

Keep your demands low today, otherwise you may find that you are not getting what you want from life. There are some great times to be had but you might have to wait for a little while in order to get the best from them. Today is best left for planning, with the real action coming a little down the line when planetary trends improve.

24 THURSDAY ☿   *Moon Age Day 2   Moon Sign Virgo*

Your efforts to get ahead in a general sense now look like bearing fruit. Your level of general energy should be slowly stepping up and there are people around you all the time now who have similar ideas to your own. There is no reason at all why you shouldn't start to regain your top form, both at work and in a social sense.

25 FRIDAY ☿ *Moon Age Day 3   Moon Sign Libra*

You are now absorbing news and views at a fantastic rate and will want to be certain that everyone knows your opinions. Good to know and great to have around, it looks as though present astrological trends are offering you one of the most potent periods you will experience during August.

26 SATURDAY ☿ *Moon Age Day 4   Moon Sign Libra*

This is a good period for useful information gathering and you won't have any difficulty being considered for advancement of some sort, be it at work or socially. Although yours is sometimes a fairly shy and retiring sort of zodiac sign, trends suggest that this will not turn out to be the case right now.

27 SUNDAY ☿ *Moon Age Day 5   Moon Sign Scorpio*

There is a zest and dynamism around at present that could easily turn out to be very infectious. It seems that you need a definite challenge and since this is a Sunday, you may have to invent one for yourself. From a physical point of view you ought to be feeling a good deal stronger than you have so far this month.

28 MONDAY ☿ *Moon Age Day 6   Moon Sign Scorpio*

You now develop very strong feelings about certain aspects of the past and will also definitely feel the need to be around people who make you feel confident. Through the whole of the recent spell of dynamic thoughts and actions, the slightly hesitant side of Pisces has been around as well and it shows even more today.

29 TUESDAY ☿ *Moon Age Day 7   Moon Sign Sagittarius*

A few of your ideas might prove to be somewhat over-ambitious and might have to fall by the wayside as a result. In the main though, you pick up one or two schemes and run with them very successfully indeed. The attitude of people you don't know very well might puzzle you unless you ask a few questions.

30 WEDNESDAY ☿ *Moon Age Day 8   Moon Sign Sagittarius*

You will discover that one-to-one relationships are the attachments you will want to explore fully around this time. You might be taking something of a holiday from the real pressures associated with work and professional matters and would be willing today to allow others to take a good deal of the strain.

31 THURSDAY ☿ *Moon Age Day 9   Moon Sign Sagittarius*

Co-operative discussions are the most productive ones for now and although there is some incentive to go it alone, this is not the right way forward. Once you get into the swing of things you should enjoy all that today has to offer and you certainly won't be inclined to stay in the shadows at any time.

September 2017

YOUR MONTH AT A GLANCE

(+) = Opportunities are around   ⬤ = Be on the defensive   ◯ = Life is pretty ordinary

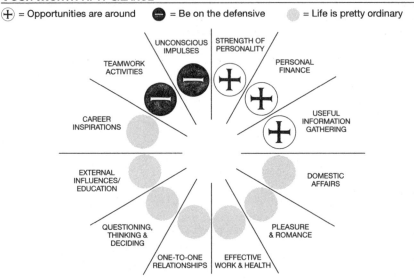

STRENGTH OF PERSONALITY

UNCONSCIOUS IMPULSES

TEAMWORK ACTIVITIES

PERSONAL FINANCE

CAREER INSPIRATIONS

USEFUL INFORMATION GATHERING

EXTERNAL INFLUENCES/ EDUCATION

DOMESTIC AFFAIRS

QUESTIONING, THINKING & DECIDING

PLEASURE & ROMANCE

ONE-TO-ONE RELATIONSHIPS

EFFECTIVE WORK & HEALTH

SEPTEMBER HIGHS AND LOWS

Here I show you how the rhythms of the Moon will affect you this month. Like the tide, your energies and abilities will rise and fall with its pattern. When it is above the centre line, go for it, when it is below, you should be resting.

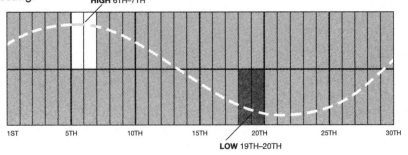

HIGH 6TH–7TH

LOW 19TH–20TH

1ST   5TH   10TH   15TH   20TH   25TH   30TH

1 FRIDAY ☿ *Moon Age Day 10   Moon Sign Capricorn*

In practical matters, there is plenty to keep you busy and you can expect a fairly good sort of day, even if not everyone is behaving in quite the way you might have expected. Keep a sense of proportion, especially when it comes to looking at matters that might involve financial decisions.

2 SATURDAY ☿ *Moon Age Day 11   Moon Sign Capricorn*

A generally agreeable period lies ahead of you. If, however, it doesn't turn out to be exciting enough for you, the chances are that you have not done all you could to pep things up. Friends are not especially predictable at this stage and there will be some leading questions to ask if you really want to know what is going on.

3 SUNDAY ☿ *Moon Age Day 12   Moon Sign Aquarius*

If your partner proves less agreeable than usual, maybe you should look for the reason within yourself. Have you forgotten an anniversary or some other important event? Have you done something wrong or been inconsiderate? Make a few kind gestures but don't go overboard as a show of obsequiousness could make matters worse.

4 MONDAY ☿ *Moon Age Day 13   Moon Sign Aquarius*

Remember there is only so much you can control on your own. The more you are willing to co-operate today, the better things are likely to go for you. Unfortunately though, it doesn't matter how hard you try, in the eyes of a very few people everything you do is wrong. Simply try to ignore anyone like this and stick with reasonable types.

5 TUESDAY ☿ *Moon Age Day 14   Moon Sign Aquarius*

In personal encounters, your competitive nature is stimulated. There's no problem here as long as your opposite number knows how to lose gracefully. It seems as though there are very few demands you would shy away from on this day but do avoid taking on more than is reasonable.

6 WEDNESDAY ☿ *Moon Age Day 15   Moon Sign Pisces*

The lunar high could easily bring a Wednesday to remember. It seems you can be an expert at just about anything now and will get jobs done whilst other stand around and stare. When it comes to winning Brownie points, days don't come much better than this one. Your prestige will be going out through the roof.

7 THURSDAY ☿ *Moon Age Day 16 Moon Sign Pisces*

Lady Luck stands behind your actions, leading to a potentially very powerful Thursday. If you are at work, put in that extra bit of effort that gets you noticed and which could make all the difference in the longer-term. On the other hand, if you can avoid work today, this would be a great time to go out and have fun.

8 FRIDAY ☿ *Moon Age Day 17 Moon Sign Aries*

The progressive phase continues and you should have plenty of power at your fingertips on those occasions you need it the most. When it comes to forward planning, you are second to none. However, it might prove propitious to give way to the ideas of your partner, or to someone you count as a really good and loyal friend.

9 SATURDAY ☿ *Moon Age Day 18 Moon Sign Aries*

If you know you are telling the truth today, it might be important to state the fact. This is necessary, even if you know you could upset someone else on the way. The problems will be much greater if you refuse to open your mouth now and will only mean some really harsh words further down the line.

10 SUNDAY ☿ *Moon Age Day 19 Moon Sign Taurus*

This is a time for spring-cleaning your life, even though this is far from being the right season. Mercury stands in good association with the Sun, making it easy for you to talk your way through necessary alterations. Meanwhile, you could find someone you love is proving to be very surprising.

11 MONDAY ☿ *Moon Age Day 20 Moon Sign Taurus*

Instinct and intuition guide you through the start of a week that requires you to react at a moment's notice. The magnetic side of your Pisces nature is now fully on display and it is clear that you are out to impress in some way. Any element of tedium in your life right now is likely to be shunned instantly in favour of action.

12 TUESDAY ☿ *Moon Age Day 21 Moon Sign Gemini*

You can enjoy a fairly high profile at the moment, particularly in social situations. It looks as though you will shine like a star when the mood takes you but on the other hand, you can be fairly sulky if you are prevailed upon to do anything that really goes against the grain. Try to avoid this as it might make you unpopular.

13 WEDNESDAY
Moon Age Day 22   Moon Sign Gemini

It is very important to be in the right place at the right time today, something you should instinctively know how to do. You should be fairly confident and not half as likely to make unforced errors as could have been the case over the last few days. If you feel anxious about a task you have to do, enlist a little support.

14 THURSDAY
Moon Age Day 23   Moon Sign Cancer

Your ability to get the best from others is quite noteworthy now. If there is something you particularly want, which can only be supplied by someone else, now is the time to turn on the charm. You could be very surprised at the reaction you get, even from people you wouldn't normally try to win round.

15 FRIDAY
Moon Age Day 24   Moon Sign Cancer

There are things happening in a career sense that you will probably enjoy a great deal. Getting on the right side of superiors should be quite easy because charm is your middle name at present. Don't go too far, though, because the actions you take have to seem both believable and sane.

16 SATURDAY
Moon Age Day 25   Moon Sign Cancer

There are influences around now that put you where the good times are. Don't be shy when it comes to showing what you are capable of doing and be willing to let your voice be heard. Although you might sometimes doubt your own abilities, in the end you are almost certain to come good.

17 SUNDAY
Moon Age Day 26   Moon Sign Leo

Things continue to go better and better on a one-to-one front. Friendship and personal relationships are very important to you at this time and you won't have any trouble bringing friends and partners round to your way of thinking. Concern for the underdog is never very far from the surface as far as you are concerned and today is no exception.

18 MONDAY
Moon Age Day 27   Moon Sign Leo

You have a real talent for communication and this is showing stronger than ever at the moment. Someone you haven't seen for a while is likely to pay a return visit to your life and could be bringing some surprises along with them. Getting to grips with a job you don't like will be quite tedious but still necessary.

19 TUESDAY
Moon Age Day 28   Moon Sign Virgo

Progress is difficult now, mainly thanks to the lunar low. If you don't try to move mountains, you will not be upset when you find it impossible to do so. Concentrate on being quiet and doing things that please only you. Spending moments on your own is not difficult and may be the best course of action today.

20 WEDNESDAY
Moon Age Day 0   Moon Sign Virgo

Only attempt today what you really know is likely to work and stay clear of any gambling or signing documents you don't really understand. If there are major purchases in the offing try to leave them until tomorrow but if that proves to be impossible, check the details very carefully and maybe take a friend along for advice.

21 THURSDAY
Moon Age Day 1   Moon Sign Libra

You have the capacity to be almost anything you would wish to be around now. Your confidence remains essentially high and there isn't much doubt about your desire to be the best. People gather round to ask your advice and what you are telling them might be at least partly appropriate for you too.

22 FRIDAY
Moon Age Day 2   Moon Sign Libra

Your social life now receives a boost. There is just a chance that you could be keener on the superficial things in life, and there doesn't appear to be much deep thinking going on. Don't worry, you manage to clock up enough hours in the average week plumbing the depths of your own Piscean nature and sometimes you really do benefit from a lighter touch.

23 SATURDAY
Moon Age Day 3   Moon Sign Scorpio

Now the Sun moves into your solar eighth house. During the next month or so you can expect the end of certain phases in your life and the beginning of new ones. This position of the Sun can also bring out the detective in you, giving you curiosity in abundance and the desire to know how everything works.

24 SUNDAY
Moon Age Day 4   Moon Sign Scorpio

The ordinary in life doesn't seem all that attractive to you at present, perhaps because things have been so exciting of late. There are tedious jobs to be done but you either get them out of the way quickly or manage to find someone to do them for you. Pisces certainly looks likely to be calling in a few favours on this particular Sunday.

25 MONDAY
Moon Age Day 5   Moon Sign Scorpio

You can be very sympathetic to the needs of those around you at the best of times but this quality is specifically emphasised at present. Consideration and concern are now your middle names. This is particularly the case with family members but friends will also be on the receiving end of your concern.

26 TUESDAY
Moon Age Day 6   Moon Sign Sagittarius

It may be time to do some serious thinking about a course of action you have taken recently. It isn't too late to modify your plans and there is no shame in doing so if you think it would suit your purposes better. Even if certain people accuse you of vacillating, what matters are your ultimate actions and successes.

27 WEDNESDAY
Moon Age Day 7   Moon Sign Sagittarius

If you have to abandon something and start again, then so be it. What you shouldn't do is to carry on regardless, even when you know that you are going in the wrong direction. Friends will offer some timely advice but don't spend all day on practical matters because there is fun to be had later.

28 THURSDAY
Moon Age Day 8   Moon Sign Capricorn

This is a very good time to socialise and to get on side with people who haven't always been your cup of tea in the past. Not everyone has the same ideas as you do and it will take time to explain your thoughts to those around you. Today has a leisurely quality that makes this process easier.

29 FRIDAY
Moon Age Day 9   Moon Sign Capricorn

Find areas and interests that make it possible to communicate with others more easily – even with people who have proved distinctly awkward in the past. Your responsibilities could get in the way today, unless you use ingenuity and variety in your thinking. Don't get stuck in a rut, even one of your own making.

30 SATURDAY
Moon Age Day 10   Moon Sign Capricorn

An emotional bond that begins to develop now should prove to be quite heart-warming in the days and weeks that lie ahead. For some Pisceans it's a whole new romantic start, whereas those of you who are settled in relationships should find them working even better for you.

October 2017

Your Month at a Glance

$\bigoplus$ = Opportunities are around $\ominus$ = Be on the defensive   ⬤ = Life is pretty ordinary

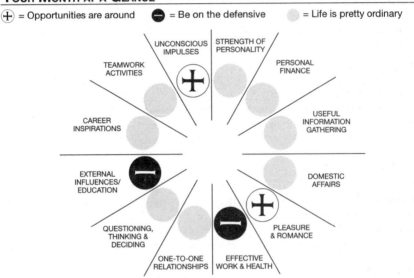

- UNCONSCIOUS IMPULSES
- STRENGTH OF PERSONALITY
- TEAMWORK ACTIVITIES
- PERSONAL FINANCE
- CAREER INSPIRATIONS
- USEFUL INFORMATION GATHERING
- EXTERNAL INFLUENCES/ EDUCATION
- DOMESTIC AFFAIRS
- QUESTIONING, THINKING & DECIDING
- PLEASURE & ROMANCE
- ONE-TO-ONE RELATIONSHIPS
- EFFECTIVE WORK & HEALTH

October Highs and Lows

Here I show you how the rhythms of the Moon will affect you this month. Like the tide, your energies and abilities will rise and fall with its pattern. When it is above the centre line, go for it, when it is below, you should be resting.

HIGH 3RD–4TH   **HIGH** 30TH–31ST

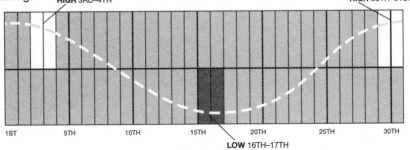

1ST   5TH   10TH   15TH   20TH   25TH   30TH

LOW 16TH–17TH

I SUNDAY
Moon Age Day I I   Moon Sign Aquarius

A personal matter is likely to put you on the defensive today but do make sure you are not defending yourself before you have even been attacked. The people who matter the most will be on your side at the moment and are unlikely to let you down, even if the going gets a little difficult.

2 MONDAY
Moon Age Day I 2   Moon Sign Aquarius

Refuse to take on any tasks or to start a completely new regime until you are sure in your own mind that present necessities are catered for. You are fairly quiet, because of a twelfth house Moon, and this period allows you to see things in stark contrast, freed from some social obligations.

3 TUESDAY
Moon Age Day I 3   Moon Sign Pisces

This is a day of high energy and maximum achievement. Catapulted out of your twelfth house moon lethargy, you now surge forward positively, making for a potentially interesting and eventful period. Confusion of any sort is blown away by a necessary and welcome wind of change.

4 WEDNESDAY
Moon Age Day I 4   Moon Sign Pisces

Getting your own way with others ought to be a piece of cake at the moment. With a natural sense of good luck, together with poise, balance and a determination to get on well, very little should be denied to you this Wednesday. The thing to avoid is staying around at home with nothing particular to do.

5 THURSDAY
Moon Age Day I 5   Moon Sign Aries

This should be a potentially wonderful time in terms of personal relationships. There are quite a few planetary aspects and positions now working in your favour and very little to get in the way of romantic bliss. If you are not involved in a personal attachment right now, perhaps you should be keeping your eyes open.

6 FRIDAY
Moon Age Day I 6   Moon Sign Aries

If you have to rethink a particular plan of action, don't see the procedure as being necessarily bad. On the contrary, the more you rush into things right now, the greater is the likelihood of making a mistake. People you haven't seen for quite some time could be making a renewed appearance in your life.

7 SATURDAY
Moon Age Day 17   Moon Sign Taurus

This may be the best time of this month to have a clear out in your life. It could be that there are certain business or social relationships that have been holding you back or people who simply don't seem to have your best interests at heart. You are far from being hard-hearted but may be forced by circumstances to look hard at situations.

8 SUNDAY
Moon Age Day 18   Moon Sign Taurus

Any outdoor pursuits you may follow are especially well highlighted now, as the more sporting and competitive side of your nature also begins to show itself. Because you are feeling somewhat brave at present, you may choose to tackle an issue that has had you quaking in your boots at some stage in the past.

9 MONDAY
Moon Age Day 19   Moon Sign Taurus

This may be the time to bring something to a successful conclusion – a possible scenario that has been around for a few days but which looks even more pertinent now. Be on the lookout for ways to improve your life and also your finances. A change of scene would probably be welcome so try to get some time out and about if you can.

10 TUESDAY
Moon Age Day 20   Moon Sign Gemini

It can benefit you greatly to keep in touch with people who are in the know. Because of your generally affable ways, people like you a great deal. Don't be afraid to turn this fact to your advantage and call in some assistance. Moving towards the culmination of plans you hatched some time ago, you should make material progress.

11 WEDNESDAY
Moon Age Day 21   Moon Sign Gemini

With a greater sense of freedom and adventure than you have experienced for some weeks, it looks as though this part of October is turning very much to your advantage. What you find within yourself right now is greater confidence and a definite desire to get on well, both practically and socially.

12 THURSDAY
Moon Age Day 22   Moon Sign Cancer

Your potential for personal freedom is very strong. This can make you something of a loose cannon on occasion because people who think they know you well are likely to be constantly surprised by your actions and reactions. It doesn't do any harm at all to keep the world guessing once in a while.

13 FRIDAY
Moon Age Day 23   Moon Sign Cancer

This is another marvellous period to get out into the world of social interaction and to make certain that your voice is heard. You will be making some new contacts today, most likely people who will become firm friends and who are in a good position to offer you some timely support.

14 SATURDAY
Moon Age Day 24   Moon Sign Leo

Social affairs should be a breeze at the moment. You have exactly what it takes to get on well with the crowd and any shyness that typifies Pisces seems to be taking a holiday for the moment. Don't be in too much of a rush to get a particular job done. It would be best to wait a while and to make sure it is done properly.

15 SUNDAY
Moon Age Day 25   Moon Sign Leo

You might have to let go of something at present if you want to make life less complicated. Perhaps you are too emotionally involved with a person or situation that is proving to be quite a problem? Whatever the difficulty might be, you can gain by putting distance between yourself and it to take some valuable thinking time.

16 MONDAY
Moon Age Day 26   Moon Sign Virgo

This certainly isn't the most progressive day of the month. The lunar low can make you feel sluggish and could see you putting off something you have been planning for a while. Make the day your own by doing exactly what takes your fancy. If that means curling up with a book, then so be it.

17 TUESDAY
Moon Age Day 27   Moon Sign Virgo

Major decisions should be left until later. You are not really in a position to take chances at the moment and might regret the fact if you do. For the moment, simply coast along and watch others setting the pace. You should be able to get a good deal from friendships and pastimes that you always enjoy.

18 WEDNESDAY
Moon Age Day 28   Moon Sign Libra

You now find yourself in a regenerative phase. The Sun is still occupying your solar eighth house, good for new starts of any sort. Active and enterprising, the lunar low has given you the time to recharge your batteries and allows you to now move forward in a very progressive way indeed.

19 THURSDAY
Moon Age Day 29   Moon Sign Libra

There could be good news coming in from far and wide, some of which you should find either exciting or at the very least joyful. Financial gains are possible, even if these seem to come despite your own best efforts and not because of them. Keep in touch with colleagues who can be of specific practical use to you.

20 FRIDAY
Moon Age Day 0   Moon Sign Libra

Much energy now seems to be going into chasing money and success. You need cash, everyone does, but this type of success might be something of an illusion, as Pisces is inclined to realise. What matters most is happiness and there should be a good deal of that around if you are willing to recognise its potential.

21 SATURDAY
Moon Age Day 1   Moon Sign Scorpio

You actively like people and enjoy the contact you have with them. This is apparent today because you will do almost anything to be amongst groups and with individuals you find interesting. What wouldn't be so comfortable for you today would be to find yourself left to your own devices and devoid of company.

22 SUNDAY
Moon Age Day 2   Moon Sign Scorpio

Making any sort of important change is likely to be quite easy today, though you may have to deal with the slightly odd behaviour of a few of the people you need to rely on at this time. Controversy is likely to touch you at some stage during the day, even if you are not the one who it is focused upon.

23 MONDAY
Moon Age Day 3   Moon Sign Sagittarius

You can get a great deal out of journeys of any sort and although the summer is now over, you might decide that the time is right to take a holiday. Travel that is organised at very short notice could be the most enjoyable of all and you can also gain from mixing with people who come from far away.

24 TUESDAY
Moon Age Day 4   Moon Sign Sagittarius

Success right now has a great deal to do with the influence you have over others. You may have to change your mind about something you thought you understood well but you won't lose credibility if you are able to explain yourself. Trends continue to suggest that controversy can dog your footsteps, perhaps in terms of your personal life.

25 WEDNESDAY
Moon Age Day 5   Moon Sign Sagittarius

Contact with a variety of different sorts of people really makes life go with a swing and you cannot afford to hide either your nature or your talents at present. If you are good at something, now is the time to show this fact to the world at large. Romance could be on the cards for both young and young-at-heart Pisceans.

26 THURSDAY
Moon Age Day 6   Moon Sign Capricorn

A personal plan or a specific intention on your part may now have to be scrapped, probably through no fault of your own. If this leads to some disappointment, the best way forward is to forget about a situation that is in the past and to push even harder for the winning post in other ways. People make a fuss of you later today.

27 FRIDAY
Moon Age Day 7   Moon Sign Capricorn

Ideas could fail to turn out quite as you had expected and that could mean being forced to alter your strategy at a moment's notice. This should not present you with too many problems, since your mind is working quickly and you don't have too much trouble thinking on your feet under present astrological trends.

28 SATURDAY
Moon Age Day 8   Moon Sign Aquarius

You should let your personality shine out this weekend because there are plenty of people watching you, some of whom are deeply attracted to that Piscean nature of yours. Don't be too modest and when you are asked for your opinion, do your best to act as though you have the right to offer it.

29 SUNDAY
Moon Age Day 9   Moon Sign Aquarius

There are planets around now that emphasise your obligations to others, which might be something of a drag during one of those few occasions for Pisces that you are thinking about yourself. It won't be long before a particularly tedious job is out of the way, which should leave you with more time to do as you please.

30 MONDAY
Moon Age Day 10   Moon Sign Pisces

There are some new and tempting ideas around at the moment and you won't be tardy when it comes to accepting an offer you seem to have been waiting for a long time. Your effectiveness at work goes without saying and you might even be able to turn heads when it comes to social situations at present.

31 TUESDAY
Moon Age Day 11   Moon Sign Pisces

This is the time when it helps to put in that extra push that can make all the difference to your situation. Some of your victories are hard won but the fact that you get there in the end is what counts. You have good persuasive powers today and shouldn't give in simply because someone seems to be saying no at first.

November
2017

YOUR MONTH AT A GLANCE

(+) = Opportunities are around   ⚫ = Be on the defensive   ⚫ = Life is pretty ordinary

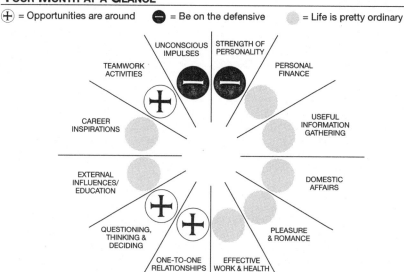

- UNCONSCIOUS IMPULSES
- STRENGTH OF PERSONALITY
- TEAMWORK ACTIVITIES
- PERSONAL FINANCE
- CAREER INSPIRATIONS
- USEFUL INFORMATION GATHERING
- EXTERNAL INFLUENCES/ EDUCATION
- DOMESTIC AFFAIRS
- QUESTIONING, THINKING & DECIDING
- PLEASURE & ROMANCE
- ONE-TO-ONE RELATIONSHIPS
- EFFECTIVE WORK & HEALTH

NOVEMBER HIGHS AND LOWS

Here I show you how the rhythms of the Moon will affect you this month. Like the tide, your energies and abilities will rise and fall with its pattern. When it is above the centre line, go for it, when it is below, you should be resting.

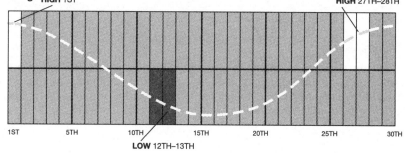

HIGH 1ST

HIGH 27TH–28TH

1ST   5TH   10TH   15TH   20TH   25TH   30TH

LOW 12TH–13TH

1 WEDNESDAY
Moon Age Day 12   Moon Sign Pisces

The start of November marks a good time for some sort of professional accomplishment. Certain matters that have been on hold for a while could well come to fruition now and the chance of making money is quite good. Other trends indicate that friends may have a special need of you around this time.

2 THURSDAY
Moon Age Day 13   Moon Sign Aries

The social highlights continue, making this a very good time for having fun and for making new friends. There are a number of confidences coming your way right now and it is very important that you guard these carefully since your reputation with some people might rest on your discretion.

3 FRIDAY
Moon Age Day 14   Moon Sign Aries

This might be a period during which you should be getting as much rest as possible. It isn't that any trends are working against your best interests but simply that you have reached the end of a particular phase and need to take a break before starting on something else. From a personal viewpoint, today should find you very content.

4 SATURDAY
Moon Age Day 15   Moon Sign Taurus

There are some new and interesting people around at the moment. If you haven't already taken this fact into account, perhaps you should do so today. Whether you meet these people at work or within your home-life, you can get a great deal out of new encounters. These should furnish you with schemes and plans for next year.

5 SUNDAY
Moon Age Day 16   Moon Sign Taurus

You can make today very interesting for yourself but there are likely to be a few small setbacks to take into account. It is possible that in the middle of enjoying yourself, there will be a number of people around who have it in mind to make you work! This really isn't the way you are feeling and even Pisces fights back sometimes.

6 MONDAY
Moon Age Day 17   Moon Sign Gemini

You are out there in the social mainstream today, even if that is not exactly where you planned on being. At every level, work takes something of a back seat, in favour of having fun. Your confidence isn't lacking, especially when you are in the company of people who naturally make you feel good.

7 TUESDAY
Moon Age Day 18   Moon Sign Gemini

It is easier to address the needs and wants of loved ones today, rather than spending too much time thinking about what you want for yourself. This is the truly unselfish quality of Pisces, which is never really very far from the surface. Your intuition works well when you are dealing with strangers.

8 WEDNESDAY
Moon Age Day 19   Moon Sign Cancer

You are in a go-ahead frame of mind but you manifest this slightly differently from usual now. If someone is needed to cheer up the 'grump of the month', then that person is definitely you. Your sense of humour is especially infectious and you have a natural wisdom that hardly anyone could fail to recognise.

9 THURSDAY
Moon Age Day 20   Moon Sign Cancer

This is a good day from a professional point of view and it is easy to make allies at every stage. A continued reliance on a specific individual could lead to one or two problems, especially if the person concerned fails to live up to your expectations. Embark on new projects with as much confidence as you can muster.

10 FRIDAY
Moon Age Day 21   Moon Sign Leo

You need to broaden your horizons as much as possible and avoid being in any way restricted in your thinking. Pisces shows itself as being very creative in terms of ideas around now, a factor that can stand you in good stead, both at home and at work. Keep abreast of current affairs as what you learn could be useful for the future.

11 SATURDAY
Moon Age Day 22   Moon Sign Leo

The opportunities for overall gain are good, though you could find yourself so keen on breaking down barriers and increasing your personal freedom that you don't address the financial aspect of life at all. Avoid listening to either rumours or gossip, both of which are highly likely to be wrong.

12 SUNDAY
Moon Age Day 23   Moon Sign Virgo

Even if you have to change direction in midstream, the fact that life is zipping along nicely is what matters the most. It is possible to see progress being made, though without feeling situations are out of control or that you have to become someone else in order to maintain the pace.

13 MONDAY
Moon Age Day 24   Moon Sign Virgo

Contacts with superiors at work might lead to a better understanding of important issues and could even prove advantageous to you personally in the fullness of time. A task to which there seems to have been no end should be drawing to a close before very long, leaving you with more time to do other things.

14 TUESDAY
Moon Age Day 25   Moon Sign Libra

It ought to be fairly easy to get your own way in personal relationships at present. All you have to do is turn on the charm and then wait to see the results. Your life is likely to be running fairly smoothly and there could be some interesting possibilities coming your way in a social sense.

15 WEDNESDAY
Moon Age Day 26   Moon Sign Libra

Variety is the spice of life, though it has to be said that you are primarily responsible for keeping things on the move at the moment. Trends suggest that an exchange of ideas could be quite illuminating and might cause you to modify your own thinking regarding a fairly important issue.

16 THURSDAY
Moon Age Day 27   Moon Sign Libra

Current trends leave you with some new directions in which to travel, either in a real or a figurative sense. Unfortunately, you might not be feeling especially brave at present but you should be able to keep this hidden so that just about everyone you meet thinks you are the bee's knees. Don't be too quick to step aside in favour of someone else.

17 FRIDAY
Moon Age Day 28   Moon Sign Scorpio

A significant intellectual boost makes itself felt around this time. Good conversation is something you really enjoy now and over the weekend and you can also have a stronger influence on the actions of your partner or family members than you might have been expecting. There are possible new rewards around most corners.

18 SATURDAY
Moon Age Day 0   Moon Sign Scorpio

You will be attending to a number of different jobs today but like the juggler you are it is possible to keep all the balls in the air at the same time. Not everyone believes in you right now but the people who matter the most will and that fact should be enough to see you through one or two potentially sticky moments.

19 SUNDAY
Moon Age Day 1   Moon Sign Sagittarius

You should find yourself on the right side of some interesting situations today, even if you have to dream them up for yourself. Not everyone displays the same sort of sense of humour that you do right now but that doesn't matter because you will make people laugh in one way or another. Look after cash in the afternoon and evening.

20 MONDAY
Moon Age Day 2   Moon Sign Sagittarius

A boost to teamwork and all co-operative ventures comes along at this time and you should make the most of these positive trends. You are getting on well with just about everyone, even if there are one or two awkward types around. Your creative potential is especially good and some of you will be thinking about redecorating.

21 TUESDAY
Moon Age Day 3   Moon Sign Sagittarius

When it comes to furthering your ambitions you are clearly second to none, even though you might have to enlist the support of others on the way. There are likely to be some unexpected events happening around this time but you should manage to deal with them relatively easily. There could be a new attachment on the way.

22 WEDNESDAY
Moon Age Day 4   Moon Sign Capricorn

Self-confidence in professional matters is clearly the way forward and you won't get anywhere at all if you fail to show those around you that you know what you are talking about. In social and family situations you are clearly putting everyone ahead of yourself, which isn't exactly unusual for Pisces.

23 THURSDAY
Moon Age Day 5   Moon Sign Capricorn

Close companions may now cause you to think quite deeply about the importance you have placed upon relationships of late. It is possible that you may decide to spend some of your social hours with people you don't see very often. This would be a good day for sending letters or for making a long-distance telephone call.

24 FRIDAY
Moon Age Day 6   Moon Sign Aquarius

New life can be breathed into situations you thought were over and done with. It is possible that someone might trust you with an important confidence and it will be of paramount importance that you keep it. Friends are likely to be particularly demanding of your time and that won't leave quite as many hours as you might have wished for practical matters.

25 SATURDAY
Moon Age Day 7   Moon Sign Aquarius

You might prove to be far too impetuous regarding the decisions you are making today and do need to think carefully about most matters. Although you might not feel you have the confidence of family members, in all probability they will back you when it really counts. Don't get involved in pointless rows.

26 SUNDAY
Moon Age Day 8   Moon Sign Aquarius

Your intuition is now much increased and it would be wise to turn it in the direction of people who are coming new into your life. These might be individuals who you meet on a professional level, or perhaps potential friends for the future. Not everything is what it seems – and it might take you a little while to work out why.

27 MONDAY
Moon Age Day 9   Moon Sign Pisces

This is definitely the time to let your light shine. There are gains to be made in just about all the areas of your life and a cheerful attitude on your part that gets you into the good books of people who really count. Personality-wise you are willing to throw caution to the wind, which makes you even more attractive.

28 TUESDAY
Moon Age Day 10   Moon Sign Pisces

You should prepare yourself for some heart-warming surprises and for a few gains that you didn't expect. Everyday matters turn up the results you have been expecting and probably more besides. With a positive and useful time ahead, you may decide to start enjoying yourself as much as you can.

29 WEDNESDAY
Moon Age Day 11   Moon Sign Aries

You can make an extremely powerful impression on those further up the tree than you are and will want to do everything you can to be noticed at the moment. There is much to be gained by being watched, even if to be so goes against the Piscean grain in one way or another. This would be a great time to take a trip.

30 THURSDAY
Moon Age Day 12   Moon Sign Aries

Avoid being too pushy at the moment because it probably won't get you very far. You need to display the humility that is part of the basic nature of your zodiac sign and then you will have everyone eating out of your hand. Your confidence grows by the moment when you are doing professional jobs you understand.

♓ December

2017

Your Month at a Glance

⊕ = Opportunities are around   ⚊ = Be on the defensive   ○ = Life is pretty ordinary

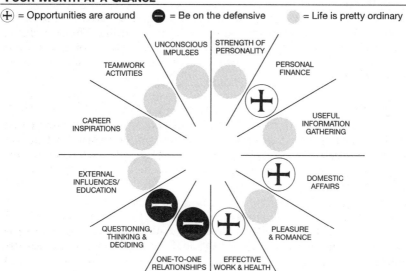

December Highs and Lows

Here I show you how the rhythms of the Moon will affect you this month. Like the tide, your energies and abilities will rise and fall with its pattern. When it is above the centre line, go for it, when it is below, you should be resting.

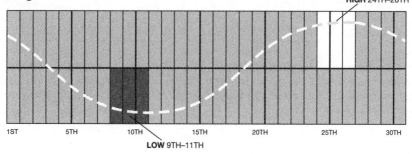

1 FRIDAY
Moon Age Day 13   Moon Sign Taurus

The things you learn from colleagues today can be of supreme importance, so it is very important to pay attention. Pisces people who are looking for work or a change of employment could also be in luck around this time. When it comes to out-of-work activities, new interests take your fancy.

2 SATURDAY
Moon Age Day 14   Moon Sign Taurus

A sense of variety and freedom is both important and appealing to Pisceans at this time. Don't be a stick-in-the-mud. Although this might not be exactly the season for outdoor activities, you should still find the lure of the wild appealing. Later in the day, you may choose to spend at least some time alone.

3 SUNDAY ☿
Moon Age Day 15   Moon Sign Gemini

Although it has occurred to you for some weeks now that Christmas is just around the corner, this is probably the first weekend you have had the chance to do much preparation for it. A shopping spree might be more fun than you would usually expect and you can also rely on the very important help of family members.

4 MONDAY ☿
Moon Age Day 16   Moon Sign Gemini

Continuing generally improving trends make themselves felt most in the workplace and in your ability to attract money. Your decision-making is good at present and you can afford to back your hunches to a greater extent. Friends should prove to be quite reliable and there are some new pals in the offing.

5 TUESDAY ☿
Moon Age Day 17   Moon Sign Cancer

An excellent day for social occasions and for getting together with the people you care for. Work might have to take something of a back seat because your mind is set firmly on having fun. Routines may be especially annoying so try to get them out of the way as early in the day as possible to make time for more interesting matters later.

6 WEDNESDAY ☿
Moon Age Day 18   Moon Sign Cancer

Don't dither or hang back when it comes to making major decisions. The more ambitious you are, the greater is your potential for success. Trends suggest that results you have been seeking for some time will be closer than you think and there is tremendous potential for doing just the right thing when it matters the most.

7 THURSDAY   ☿   *Moon Age Day 19   Moon Sign Leo*

The planetary emphasis falls on finances, which might be handy considering this expensive time of year. You are quite canny at the moment and know full well how to get value for money. Even well in advance of the traditional sales, you might be able to search out one or two things for Christmas at rock-bottom prices.

8 FRIDAY   ☿   *Moon Age Day 20   Moon Sign Leo*

A fast pace of events in the professional or practical world is probably what you can expect today. There is vital information there for the taking and you won't be slow to pick up on what others are trying to tell you. Give yourself a pat on the back for a recent personal success but don't allow it to go to your head.

9 SATURDAY   ☿   *Moon Age Day 21   Moon Sign Virgo*

You now have to put up with the last lunar low of the year, though for a host of astrological reasons you might fail to even register its presence now. You have great momentum and can whizz through difficult moments almost without noticing them. Trends do send a warning, however, to be wary of someone you know and remember that not everyone is trustworthy.

10 SUNDAY   ☿   *Moon Age Day 22   Moon Sign Virgo*

The slack pace of progress might annoy you, though there is a good chance that you won't lose too much momentum, or alternatively that it won't bother you at all because you are in a relaxed Sunday mood. There isn't much doubt about the Piscean desire to enjoy itself right now.

11 MONDAY   ☿   *Moon Age Day 23   Moon Sign Virgo*

Some of the things that are happening around you at present seem less fulfilling. Tackle this by broadening your horizons and not allowing yourself to be intimidated by little setbacks. The lunar low doesn't really help the situation but whether or not you enjoy what today has on offer seems to be up to you.

12 THURSDAY   ☿   *Moon Age Day 24   Moon Sign Libra*

As you grow more and more confident after the lunar low, so you are less intimidated by finding yourself in the limelight. It is true that others will be making a fuss of you at the moment and you are likely to make the most of the situation. Today is also very good for all aspects of romance and one-to-one encounters.

13 WEDNESDAY ☿   *Moon Age Day 25   Moon Sign Libra*

If you try to take on too many diverse interests today this could prove to be a mistake. You would be much better off concentrating on one thing at a time and avoiding unnecessary mistakes. A methodical and steady approach could lead to success, leaving plenty of time in which to enjoy yourself.

14 THURSDAY ☿   *Moon Age Day 26   Moon Sign Scorpio*

This would be a good time to take a short break and to mull over your present successes. You might not be able to see everything in its true light just at the moment but where it matters the most you begin to see a chink of light at the end of the tunnel. Friends will demand your time and you will be happy to help if you can.

15 FRIDAY ☿   *Moon Age Day 27   Moon Sign Scorpio*

The quickening of the pace around you in everyday life is now very obvious and you will barely have time to breathe right now. Don't leave travel plans to chance but make sure that all details are sorted well in advance of any journey you intend to take this week or perhaps during the Christmas break.

16 SATURDAY ☿   *Moon Age Day 28   Moon Sign Scorpio*

A boost to all social matters comes along and it looks as though you are already getting yourself into a Christmas frame of mind. All is happiness around you and if you have been a little restricted by the negative attitude of friends or family members, this sort of situation is now likely to be disappearing.

17 SUNDAY ☿   *Moon Age Day 29   Moon Sign Sagittarius*

Intellectual inspiration comes your way through conversations with people socially, or perhaps through travel. It seems that others find you extremely entertaining to have around and they could be making you feel like a celebrity at the moment. Confidences come in thick and fast, some of them from directions you certainly would not have expected.

18 MONDAY ☿   *Moon Age Day 0   Moon Sign Sagittarius*

Some people might describe you as being too assertive at present but if they do it's probably only because they are used to getting their own way. All that is happening is that you know what you want from life and are presently willing to say so. Avoid getting into pointless discussions about things that don't matter.

19 TUESDAY ☿ *Moon Age Day 1   Moon Sign Capricorn*

This can be an especially rewarding day for many Pisceans, a situation that is brought about as a result of a cocktail of positive planetary positions. You are able to confirm one or two suspicions regarding someone you haven't trusted for a while but in the main you find others to be reliable and helpful.

20 WEDNESDAY ☿ *Moon Age Day 2   Moon Sign Capricorn*

Venus is now in your solar twelfth house and this causes you to reassess the effect you have on those around you. This is likely to be a generally positive process but you are inclined to doubt yourself on occasion and this tendency does show. Stay as positive as you can about all issues that arise today.

21 THURSDAY ☿ *Moon Age Day 3   Moon Sign Capricorn*

It could become quite clear that a change in attitude is necessary when it comes to personal attachments. Maybe your partner is behaving in a slightly odd way and it's up to you to discover why this might be. Getting ahead in any practical sense is not likely today and this could be somewhat frustrating.

22 FRIDAY ☿ *Moon Age Day 4   Moon Sign Aquarius*

Right now you should be enjoying high points in love and romantic affairs, not to mention receiving a definite boost to your ego that comes from a number of different directions. You clearly believe in yourself and while this is the case you won't be short of ideas or ways in which you can make them work out as you would wish.

23 SATURDAY *Moon Age Day 5   Moon Sign Aquarius*

Faces old and new come along now, immediately ahead of the Christmas period. You might be deliberately taking a trip down memory lane at some stage today because that is what Christmas is all about. With only a few days to go, most Pisceans should now be pleased with the arrangements they have made.

24 SUNDAY *Moon Age Day 6   Moon Sign Pisces*

Your potential for lucky breaks is greater than usual on this Christmas Eve and you won't be inclined to look on the negative side of any situation at present. It should be easy to pull in a favour or two and your general level of popularity seems higher than ever. In reality, you are always popular but you realise it more at this time.

25 MONDAY
Moon Age Day 7   Moon Sign Pisces

What could be better than a lunar high that coincides with Christmas Day? It makes you bright and breezy and gives you all the energy you could possibly need to get through a busy schedule. If there is time to slump on the sofa after lunch, so much the better but you probably won't feel the need for this whilst in your present mood.

26 TUESDAY
Moon Age Day 8   Moon Sign Pisces

Getting into heated debates could be more enjoyable than you might imagine and with the lunar high still present, you are hardly likely to lose. Back your hunches to the hilt and do what you can to make progress your middle name. You can also take time out in order to simply enjoy the day.

27 WEDNESDAY
Moon Age Day 9   Moon Sign Aries

This is a time for enjoying the company of others for its own sake. You appear to have no agenda whatsoever today and so this might be an excellent time to simply be yourself. This is a concept that is more understandable to Pisces than any of the other twelve zodiac signs.

28 THURSDAY
Moon Age Day 10   Moon Sign Aries

You can capitalise on new opportunities and won't be stuck when it comes to expressing your opinions, no matter who is on the receiving end. Although you might not have too much professional influence at the moment, there are ideas coming into your mind right now that you will act upon after the New Year.

29 FRIDAY
Moon Age Day 11   Moon Sign Taurus

Variety is clearly the spice of life and you are likely to have more and more energy, even though the holidays might put a dampener on the sort of progress you want to make. You are torn between personal enjoyment and the ability to make a real impression on life and will have to exercise some true Piscean patience.

30 SATURDAY
Moon Age Day 12   Moon Sign Taurus

This should be a fairly brisk time socially and you will almost certainly notice some of the recent frustrations now disappearing. Your confidence is still strong and you remain willing to suspend some actions until next week. As a result there is more time available to simply enjoy yourself in the company of family and friends.

31 SUNDAY
Moon Age Day 13   Moon Sign Gemini

Don't get too tied up with details because it is clearly the overall picture that is important at present. A job you have been involved with for quite some time could be nearly over but once again you might have to shelve such matters as the end of the year celebrations take over. This ought to be a very enjoyable time.

How to Calculate Your Rising Sign

Most astrologers agree that, next to the Sun Sign, the most important influence on any person is the Rising Sign at the time of their birth. The Rising Sign represents the astrological sign that was rising over the eastern horizon when each and every one of us came into the world. It is sometimes also called the Ascendant.

Let us suppose, for example, that you were born with the Sun in the zodiac sign of Libra. This would bestow certain characteristics on you that are likely to be shared by all other Librans. However, a Libran with Aries Rising would show a very different attitude towards life, and of course relationships, than a Libran with Pisces Rising.

For these reasons, this book shows how your zodiac Rising Sign has a bearing on all the possible positions of the Sun at birth. Simply look through the Aries table opposite.

As long as you know your approximate time of birth the graph will show you how to discover your Rising Sign.

Look across the top of the graph of your zodiac sign to find your date of birth, and down the side for your birth time (I have used Greenwich Mean Time). Where they cross is your Rising Sign. Don't forget to subtract an hour (or two) if appropriate for Summer Time.

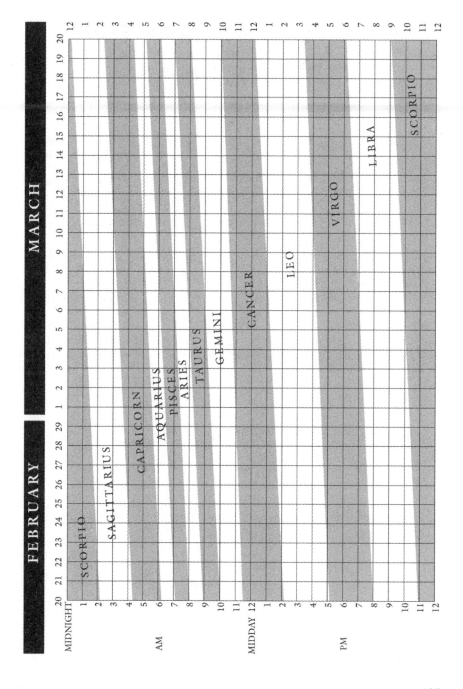

THE ZODIAC, PLANETS AND CORRESPONDENCES

The Earth revolves around the Sun once every calendar year, so when viewed from Earth the Sun appears in a different part of the sky as the year progresses. In astrology, these parts of the sky are divided into the signs of the zodiac and this means that the signs are organised in a circle. The circle begins with Aries and ends with Pisces.

Taking the zodiac sign as a starting point, astrologers then work with all the positions of planets, stars and many other factors to calculate horoscopes and birth charts and tell us what the stars have in store for us.

The table below shows the planets and Elements for each of the signs of the zodiac. Each sign belongs to one of the four Elements: Fire, Air, Earth or Water. Fire signs are creative and enthusiastic; Air signs are mentally active and thoughtful; Earth signs are constructive and practical; Water signs are emotional and have strong feelings.

It also shows the metals and gemstones associated with, or corresponding with, each sign. The correspondence is made when a metal or stone possesses properties that are held in common with a particular sign of the zodiac.

Finally, the table shows the opposite of each star sign – this is the opposite sign in the astrological circle.

Placed	Sign	Symbol	Element	Planet	Metal	Stone	Opposite
1	Aries	Ram	Fire	Mars	Iron	Bloodstone	Libra
2	Taurus	Bull	Earth	Venus	Copper	Sapphire	Scorpio
3	Gemini	Twins	Air	Mercury	Mercury	Tiger's Eye	Sagittarius
4	Cancer	Crab	Water	Moon	Silver	Pearl	Capricorn
5	Leo	Lion	Fire	Sun	Gold	Ruby	Aquarius
6	Virgo	Maiden	Earth	Mercury	Mercury	Sardonyx	Pisces
7	Libra	Scales	Air	Venus	Copper	Sapphire	Aries
8	Scorpio	Scorpion	Water	Pluto	Plutonium	Jasper	Taurus
9	Sagittarius	Archer	Fire	Jupiter	Tin	Topaz	Gemini
10	Capricorn	Goat	Earth	Saturn	Lead	Black Onyx	Cancer
11	Aquarius	Waterbearer	Air	Uranus	Uranium	Amethyst	Leo
12	Pisces	Fishes	Water	Neptune	Tin	Moonstone	Virgo